D1558685

Romance in the Ivory Tower

Other Books by Paul R. Abramson

Personality: A Heuristic Perspective
Sarah: A Sexual Biography
Bias in Psychotherapy (edited with Joan Murray)
A Case for Case Studies
With Pleasure: Thoughts on the Nature of Human Sexuality (with Steve Pinkerton)
Sexual Nature/Sexual Culture (edited with Steve Pinkerton)
A House Divided: Suspicions of Mother-Daughter Incest (with Steve Pinkerton)
Sexual Rights in America: The Ninth Amendment and the Pursuit of Happiness (with Steve Pinkerton and Mark Huppin)

Romance in the Ivory Tower

The Rights and Liberty of Conscience

Paul R. Abramson

The MIT Press
Cambridge, Massachusetts
London, England

For information about special quantity discounts, please e-mail ⟨special_sales@mitpress.mit.edu⟩.

This book was set in Sabon on 3B2 by Asco Typesetters, Hong Kong. Printed on recycled paper and bound in the United States of America.

Library of Congress Cataloging-in-Publication Data

Abramson, Paul R., 1949–
Romance in the ivory tower : the rights and liberty of conscience / Paul R. Abramson.
    p.   cm.
Includes bibliographical references and index.
ISBN 978-0-262-01237-9 (hardcover : alk. paper)
1. Freedom of expression—United States. 2. Liberty of conscience—United States. I. Title.
KF4770.A93   2007
342.7308'58—dc22   2007002119

10   9   8   7   6   5   4   3   2   1

To my wife, Ann, as love is love's reward

Contents

Acknowledgments

Some authors have perfected the art of writing. Carefully crafted sentences flow from their fingers, fitting seamlessly, or better yet miraculously, into an organized book.

I, however, am not one of them. My books are more like sculpting with clay. They transform constantly, with chunks getting added or sliced off. Nothing fully materializes until the end.

Thus, to me, perhaps more than most, I appreciate the comments of reviewers. I'd now like to recognize and thank them for such. The following people added immeasurably to the final product in one way or another: Ralph Bolton, Nick Grossman, Keith Holyoak, John Melack, Ben Pettit, Steve Pinkerton, Don Symons, two anonymous reviewers, and last but not least, my editor at The MIT Press, Clay Morgan. To all of you I give my thanks.

Romance in the Ivory Tower

Introduction

"I believe the best teaching is done in bed," Allen Ginsberg declared.

"Are you serious?" asked the *Washington Post* reporter.

"I'm totally serious. . . . It's healthy and appropriate for the student and teacher to have a love relationship whenever possible. Obviously the teacher can't have a love relationship with everyone in the class and the student can't have a love relationship with everyone of the teachers, because this is strictly human business where some people are attracted to others, but where there is that possibility, I think it should be institutionally encouraged."[1]

Whether apocryphal or not, Ginsberg's perspective reflects a certain reality. There are professors who routinely engage in sexual relationships with their students. Ginsberg, apparently, was one of them.

Rather than encouraging faculty-student romances, as championed by Ginsberg, many universities have now adopted a policy that prohibits romantic relationships between professors and students (e.g., "for whom a professor currently or prospectively might have academic responsibility"). Professors who fail to abide by this policy face employment termination.

This book examines the propriety of professor-student romance. Despite the two aforementioned points of view, the fundamental inquiry, I believe, is not whether campus romance should be encouraged or prohibited but whether the *choice* to engage in a campus romance should be *protected* or precluded. Meaning, simply, that who sleeps with whom on U.S. college campuses is secondary to the question of where the power to make the choice resides.

After my own university (the University of California at Los Angeles) announced its ban on romantic relationships between professors and students, I began to wonder whether romance was truly within the province of the academy? By what authority, I questioned, did the university become the arbiter of romantic etiquette among consenting adults?

Although on-campus romance is trivial in the big scheme of things, the resurrection of many essential constitutional rights has been precipitated by reactions to ordinary events. Sitting on a bus (Rosa Parks; civil rights), using a condom (*Griswold v. Connecticut*; the right of privacy), and drinking beer outside a bar (*Bowers v. Hardwick*; homosexual rights) are prototypical examples. It was thus wise, I thought, not to dismiss romance in the ivory tower simply because it was facile to do so.

Give the Pervert a Chance

Rhetoric aside, perhaps championing this cause is simply a form of self-justification. I raise this issue for a specific reason. I believe that anyone who ventures into these waters is presumed to have a vested interest in doing so. Here is my evidence.

Though the subject of this book is by no means a central focus of my work, I have in fact written about this topic once previously. It was a commentary titled "No More Amour with

UC Faculty," published in the *Los Angeles Times* (June 18, 2003). The editorial was a challenge to the recent University of California prohibition against faculty-student romance.

What was remarkable about this experience was an inter-office *Los Angeles Times* memo that was inadvertently sent to me during the editorial review process. Just below the e-mail accepting my commentary was an earlier e-mail, circulated solely among the *Los Angeles Times* editors, asking whether we should "give the pervert a chance."

The "pervert," it turns out, was me!

Having discovered the e-mail, I sent the editor the following reply (June 17, 2003). My intent, admittedly, was to be light-hearted, but at the same time to assure the editor that the piece had no bearing on my existing personal life. I include it herein because it is perhaps relevant to the readers of this book as well.

In working on the editing of "An Ode to Love at UCLA" [my original title] I noticed an interoffice e-mail questioning whether we should "give the pervert chance." The pervert, it seems, was in reference to me. I was both surprised and amused.

I am assuming, in the first place, that it was a joke—and certainly not for my eyes. Having seen it, however, I thought I'd give a short reply. Protesting too much being patently counterproductive.

I am, undoubtedly, a "pervert" to some. Teaching or writing about human sexuality alone would warrant the label. However, since you plan on publishing my piece, I decided to tell you a little bit more about myself.

If I can trust my memory, say, for at least the past twenty years, I have never dated (sexual or otherwise) a student of mine [or under my supervision] at UCLA. Now, being 53, I am more likely to evoke mental pictures of "grandpa" rather than romance, certainly among [most] female undergraduates. I'm a dad (2 daughters, 13 and 9); am in a monogamous relationship (monogamy, certainly to me, being an essential ingredient for trust and intimacy); and am probably better known in my community as a soccer coach than professor.

I came to write about constitutional law after twenty-five years of being an expert witness in sex-related cases (throughout the United States). Since many of the civil lawsuits involved multimillion dollar settlements, I've been spied on, repeatedly, by private investigators, hoping to find some perv stuff to get me disqualified (or embarrassed) as an expert witness. To date, nothing emerged, suggesting, at the very least, that I'm discrete, if not white bread.

In closing, I thought I'd share [a description of] an interaction with my daughter when she was in the fifth grade. We were arguing about her math homework. I was suggesting that she solve the problem in manner A; she argued for manner B. I protested that I was "a teacher; a professor." She replied, "What do you know about math? You teach sex."

Not quite pervert. But in the vicinity.

The editor (and various bosses) sent urgent (and profuse) apologies, stating among many things that it was simply a "stupid joke." I accepted their explanations at face value, noting that the *Los Angeles Times* is "hardly the first institution to poke fun at sex researchers." The issue was thus resolved amicably.

But the *Los Angeles Times* was not alone in questioning my motives. I soon discovered that a reviewer of an early draft of this book had a similar reaction. The reviewer concluded that I was someone with a "personal ax to grind." After thirty years as a sex researcher (and expert witness in criminal, civil, and constitutional litigation involving sex), I am used to ad hominem attacks—which unfortunately seem to come with the territory. An interest in sex is considered healthy, but a *scientific* interest in human sexuality is considered, at least among some people, a perversion.

The College Campus

Returning now to the focus of this book, I want to concede, as a first step, that faculty-student romance brings problems to the table. Two issues stand out as being critical: the status (and power) imbalance, and the potential for favoritism. Both issues invariably emerge as purportedly compelling justifications for prohibiting such liaisons.

The first question, then, is whether they are in fact valid concerns, and second, whether they represent sufficient justifications for prohibiting the relationships in the first place.

These concerns, to say the least, are patently self-evident. To argue otherwise is absurd. Students and professors occupy very different roles on a college campus that correspond to dissimilar sources of power and status. Professors rule, so to speak. Students do not.

Second, it is specious to claim that we do not favor those with whom we are romantically entangled. Favoritism is at the heart of romanticism. We cherish those we love. Alternatively, it is equally reasonable for students who are not romantically involved with their professors to raise concerns about being disadvantaged in comparison to those students who are. Academia is a fiercely competitive environment, and students want to compete on a level playing field.

Conceding the validity of these concerns, the next question is whether they are sufficient grounds to prohibit romantic relationships between professors and students in the first place. This is where the debate begins.

Opinions, not unexpectedly, are extraordinarily divided, in both the general and academic literatures (see the *Chronicle of Higher Education* for an overview).[2] *Yale Magazine*, for example, deplored such relationships in an article on "risky romance."[3] Jane Gallop, on the other hand, makes it clear in her book *Accused of Sexual Harassment* that professor-student romance is here to stay.[4]

Even the American Association of University Professors (AAUP) and the American Civil Liberties Union (ACLU) have vastly different points of view. The AAUP, for instance, in its policy recommendations on sexual harassment concludes that *consensual* sexual relationships between professors and students are "fraught" with difficulties, and as such, that when they exist, "effective steps should be taken to ensure unbiased evaluation or supervision of the student."[5]

The ACLU president, Nadine Strossen, begs to differ. When sexual harassment policy is extended to consensual sexual relations, Strossen believes that it is simply "a Trojan horse" designed to smuggle antisex views into law and culture.[6]

The legal literature, not surprisingly, is no less divided. There are many authors who abhor faculty-student romance, asserting foremost that the power differential precludes consent.[7] There are also, predictably, other authors who vigorously defend these relationships.[8] The reader is well advised to review these writings too.

The controversies in the academic and legal literatures notwithstanding, many universities and colleges (e.g., Yale University, the College of William and Mary, the University of Iowa, etc.) have now made the preemptive decision to prohibit faculty-student romance (in one form or another). These prohibitions are far from benign, containing various duties and sanctions, including the threat of employment termination.

Yet I do not believe that the proffered justifications for such policies are sufficient enough to offset the right of consenting adults to make choices within this intimate area of personal autonomy. Why?

Though professors and students occupy very different positions of status and power, the important question, to me at least, is whether that status differential should preclude a romantic relationship in the first place. In the best of all worlds, every couple would consist of partners of equal status, power, age, attractiveness, and so forth, so that it would be an equal partnership in every way and form. But is this realistic?

If, in the real world, relationship imbalances exist (age, status, salary, attractiveness, or whatever), why has the university decided that it must now legislate against them? What if hospitals determined that doctors could not be romantically involved with nurses? Or what if the government proclaimed that judges and senators must be romantically involved with like-status partners, given their inherent power (and the manner in which it would pervade the relationship)? Other examples would suffice as well, but the point is simply that many relationships have a fundamental imbalance, and either survive or perish as a result. They are not, however, prohibited in the first place—certainly not if the partners are consenting adults and the relationship is void of tangible harm.

Romance on a Therapist's Couch

There is, of course, an exception to this: namely, a sexual relationship between a psychotherapist and their client. Depending on the jurisdiction, sex between a psychotherapist and a client can be a criminal offense, or grounds for revoking a professional license. It is also deemed, not surprisingly, a violation of professional ethics.

The big question, then, is whether sex between a psychotherapist and a client is the same as sex between a professor and a student, and if so, are equivalent sanctions applicable?

Three possible reasons exist for precluding sex between a psychotherapist and a client: the client's attributes; the psychotherapist's attributes; and the attributes of the psycho-therapeutic relationship itself.[9]

It is often argued that therapist-client sex is prohibited because the client, by virtue of the need for psychotherapy, is in a state of diminished capacity. Accordingly, the client is not capable of providing informed consent to sex with their therapist.

There are, unfortunately, a number of problems with this rationale. Foremost is the fact that we presume, as a matter of law, that most clients are still capable of giving consent to all other aspects of their lives, notably including the therapy itself, the therapy fee structure, and sex with someone other than the therapist. Clearly, we do not operate on the assumption that most clients in therapy lack the capacity to consent.

Perhaps, then, it is not the client's attributes but alternatively the attributes of the psychotherapist that elicits disapprobation. For example, therapists are for the most part highly educated, professionally trained, licensed, and financially secure—characteristics that are perhaps unduly seductive to clients. Yet curiously, we do not prohibit these very same clients from engaging in sexual relationships with other individuals of wealth, education, and status. These characteristics alone cannot obviously be the basis for the exclusion.

It is, instead, the nature of the psychotherapy relationship that warrants the prohibition. Of particular relevance are the following attributes. Psychotherapy is initiated by a psychologically vulnerable client, who speaks on the condition of confidentiality about intimate issues, void of joint self-revelation, in an environment controlled completely by the therapist.[10] On top of this, the relationship also contains transference, the process whereby the client projects emotionally significant attributes on to the therapist. Psychotherapy, in fact, utilizes the transference as part of the treatment of the client.

Returning now to the initial question, the crux of the matter is whether the professor-student relationship is equivalent to that of the psychotherapist-client one, so much so that the prohibitions are similarly justified.

The answer, at least according to Sherry Young, an authority in this field, is absolutely not. Young asserts that you'd have to stretch the analogy "to the point of absurdity" to make this fit.[11]

Why? Suffice it to say that the institutional parameters of psychotherapy, including transference, initial psychological vulnerability, unilateral self-revelation, and so forth, are not by any means integral to the romantic relationships between professors and students.

Playing Favorites

What about favoritism?

I am much more sympathetic to this concern. It is difficult (perhaps impossible) to avoid favoring those we love. To claim otherwise, I believe, is untenable. Even if it were occasionally true that a professor could remain thoroughly objective with every student regardless of a romantic attachment, no one would believe it anyway.

But the critical question, at least to me, is whether this is a sufficient justification to prohibit romantic relationships between professors and students. Here is where it gets complicated.

Take college athletics. Does favoritism lurk therein? Are athletes, for example, favored in college admissions, whereby athleticism offsets academic shortcomings? What about athletic scholarships and tutoring programs? Are college athletes the recipients of preferential treatment there as well?

I believe it is naive, to say the least, to contend that college athletes are not the recipients of institutional favoritism, especially when it is strikingly more pervasive than the prospect of a romantically smitten college professor unduly inflating the evaluation of their lover. Romanced students may accrue favoritism, but athletes are uniformly the campus darlings.

Here is another issue to consider. What about the process by which we ensure diversity on campus? Does it promote favoritism too?

Take, for instance, the minority professor who reaches out to minority students, creating support groups, which eventually include weekly entertaining at the professor's home. Surely this professor will think favorably of their students. Yet we do not prohibit such relationships based on concerns related to potential favoritism. The same would be obviously true of all mentoring relationships, such as working in a professor's lab and so on. When people get close, for whatever reason, they tend to favor each other.[12]

Now given that favoritism exists on college campuses, it seems reasonable to ask whether we need to isolate and *prohibit* a specific class of relationships (professor-student romance) where the potential for favoritism resides when alternative remedies exist as well?

A *conflict of interest* policy, for example, is a far more compelling and judicious solution to this conundrum of potential favoritism among romancing professors and students than the prevailing institutional prohibitions. There is a sizable literature, legal and otherwise, on this strategy. The basic principle is to eliminate impartiality. Judges, for instance, must disqualify themselves in cases where a personal bias exists (e.g., a former partnership with a prevailing attorney). Medical researchers must disclose all sources of funding, particularly from drug manufacturers. Professors who are romantically involved with their students, I believe, share the same potential for impartiality, and would benefit from similar procedures for mitigating conflicts of interest (e.g., recusal, disclosure, and third-party evaluations). If a student falls in love with a supervising professor, the simplest strategy to avoid the appearance of impartiality is to switch professors (or classes). When this is not feasible, however, it seems equally reasonable to involve a third-party evaluator. The professor could ask a colleague or teaching assistant, say, to perform all evaluative functions of the student. Though these solutions are not without limitations, they are at the very least completely in line with those employed in other circumstances where the potential for impartiality prevails. Such strategies thereby address the legitimate concerns raised previously about undue favoritism, without capsizing cherished freedoms, such as the choice of whom to love. More on this topic will follow.

Back to Romance

Other nuances of faculty-student romance also deserve mention. For example, in many types of courses there are no letter grades (but simply pass or no pass), especially in graduate school. Other forms of collaboration exist (which are technically supervisory) where no grading whatsoever is apparent, such as when a professor and a student write a paper together. The current policies prohibiting faculty-student romance make no distinction between graded (where being impartial is severely constrained) and nongraded academic responsibilities. This issue is significant because, as it turns out, the nongraded academic responsibilities are of a longer duration (oftentimes years) than the graded ones (which usually last no more than ten to twelve weeks).

At the heart of this debate, certainly among those with an open mind, is not so much the concern over whether professors should be sexually involved with students in their (traditional) classes but instead the blanket prohibition against romantic involvement with a student "for whom a professor currently or *prospectively* might have academic responsibility." In most doctoral programs, this could be a six-year moratorium against romantic involvement with someone you love. It is perhaps the proverbial "burning down the house to roast the pig." If the purpose is to ensure that a professor does not give an inflated grade, an alternative policy, like third-party evaluation, might once again suffice.

There are, of course, other complaints about faculty-student romance (e.g., it is disruptive to the teaching mission, it gives the college a bad name, and so forth). These too, I believe, are legitimate concerns, but not sufficient enough for prohibiting romantic liaisons.

On the other hand, one might also argue that the benefits of such relationships (emotionally, intellectually, etc.) outweigh all attempts to prohibit them. Ginsberg, for example, claimed that having sex with a student resulted in better poetry. Whether Ginsberg was being disingenuous or merely amusing himself with the reporter is unknown. He may have been completely sincere. In any case, it seems apparent that faculty-student romances generally do little tangible harm, while offering the potential for profound emotional benefits to both partners.

Provided they are consensual and void of coercion, these relationships, in my view, do not warrant criminal sanctions nor the status of actionable "offenses," university prohibitions notwithstanding, particularly given the various options for alternative forms of grading (e.g., third-party involvement, etc.).

Where, then, does that leave us? Is it really worth the trouble of overturning university policy simply to allow professors and students to fall in love or have sex? Do we need a campaign, as unsavory as it sounds, to bring free love back to the ivory tower?

If this were simply about free love, I would have to say no, it's not worth the trouble. But I believe that a more fundamental right is at stake. At the center of the issue is a simple question: Do we, as consenting adults, have a constitutional right to make intimate choices (void of tangible harm), such as who to romance?

The Rights of Conscience

I have something more universal in mind than the question of whether students should be permitted to romance their professors, or vice versa. It is something germane to all the deeply personal choices we make—namely, the *rights of conscience.* That is, the right we rely on when making choices relevant to personal autonomy, with the belief in God being a prime example.

Outrage, no doubt, would emerge if an institution prohibited the belief in God. God is a deeply personal matter outside the reach of a university. It is my position that we should be no less indignant when a university prohibits who we can romance (presuming, of course, that the partnership involves consenting adults in a relationship void of tangible harm).

On what basis do I make this claim?

First, I maintain that the Ninth Amendment ("The enumeration in the Constitution, of certain rights, shall not be construed to deny or disparage others retained by the people") protects the "right to romance." The government obviously is not the fountainhead of romantic alignments. Romance, instead, is a quintessential right retained by the people. It is no less essential to our well-being and happiness, I assert, than the freedom of speech. It is in fact hard to imagine liberty without either right. Furthermore, the right to *choose* a romantic partner is the prerequisite right to romance itself. Romantic choice is therefore the vehicle by which we exercise romantic freedom.[13]

Second, and more notably, I hold that our right to romance is a fundamental right of conscience. This is both a moral and legal contention. The strength of this belief, however, does not depend on the specifics. Slavery, discrimination, and so forth are universally unjust whether supported or prohibited by law. Some things, clearly, are patently right, and some things, similarly, are patently wrong. Having sole personal discretion over the choice of whom to romance, I believe, falls into the former. Hopefully, the arguments presented in this book will help make that apparent.

I am extolling the rights of conscience (in conjunction with the Ninth Amendment) because such rights represent the constitutional bedrock that supports our religious rights and, more generally, all rights made within the personal dominion of intimate choice. The belief in God is no less critical to who we are, then are the beliefs we have about romance. Denying the right to express romance because of an inherent difference in status is no less of a compelling argument then denying the right to express a religious belief that is different from a traditional U.S. norm. It may not be the type of relationship or religion we prefer, but that choice, fortunately in the United States, is assigned to one's individual conscience.

In order to fully appreciate this perspective one must comprehend the basis by which religious choice is protected in the United States. Understanding that dynamic will facilitate an appreciation of the broader implications of the rights of conscience in general as well as their applicability to the choice of who to romance and how romance is expressed.

But first I want to introduce a word of caution. Though the political rhetoric about the freedom of religion is ever present, the constitutional basis of this profound liberty is only vaguely understood. In order to grasp the commonality among all the fundamental choices we make, religion and romance among them, we must begin by examining why the rights of conscience matter in the first place, and why such rights play an important role in religion and beyond. Without an appreciation of this history and perspective, it is difficult to understand why it worthwhile to protest against the prohibitions governing faculty-student romance.

Religion is the mainstay of U.S. politics and the talisman of political ascent. Nothing apparently wields as much political power as the word of God. This is particularly true of presidential elections, whereby religion routinely bludgeons political rivals.

Why is religion important in the politics of the United States? The reasoning goes something like this. This country was built on a foundation of religion. Early Americans (at least those of European descent) arrived in Massachusetts seeking freedom from religious persecution. When the United States itself was created, the founders were deeply religious as well. The First Amendment to the Constitution protects religious freedom, religion is well integrated into national rituals, and many U.S. citizens believe that religion is the ultimate moral measure of most things American.

All of this may be true, but it is hardly the whole story. Conveniently omitted from this narrative is the explicit constitutional language forbidding a national religion or the use of religious devotion (or affiliation) as criteria for political office. Separating religion from the government was unquestionably paramount to the founders, who though religious, also feared the power of religion, particularly if institutionalized at the federal level. The Constitution protects the individual rights of citizens to worship in accordance with their own conscience, while at the same time providing safeguards against the tyranny of religious majorities.

Protection against the "tyranny of the majority" is a central theme in the writings of Thomas Jefferson and James Madison, and is not limited to religion alone. The majority is always a threat to individual liberties, whether religious or secular. In the present book I suggest that the historical significance of religious freedom in the United States per se has been vastly overstated and has failed to recognize that religious freedom was simply the handmaiden to the *liberty* of conscience. Or to put it another way, religious choice is simply one example of a *right* of conscience, no more privileged than any other, with all such rights being protected—from the majority and other encroachments—in the service of *individual* choice.

Why is this distinction important? It is crucial (not the least of which for the present purposes) because it emphasizes that all freedoms, religion included, were designed to protect the right to think and judge freely—meaning, basically, that it is the *freedom to make choices* that matters the most. Whether one chooses to believe in religion, make a political speech, keep firearms, or fall in love (or lust) is clearly secondary to the right and privilege to make those choices in the first place.

The big question, then, is what constitutes the point of origin—meaning, specifically, where do these choices, or the rights to judge and think, originate? Is it in the Bible or the U.S. Constitution? Perhaps it is neither, but instead simply the nature of the human brain and the neurophysiology of consciousness and cognition.

While the latter may be true, it is hardly what the founders had in mind. They undoubtedly debated the relative influence of God, nature, crowns of state, ruling governments, and the self, trying at some level to answer who or what is pulling the strings, and who or what gets to decide?

Their conclusion, interestingly, was no less of a revolution then the War of Independence itself. Despite all the purported religious fervor among early Americans, the founders concluded that the source of personal determination was not God or the specific guidelines of a religious text such as the Bible but instead something more down to earth: the individual self, in accordance with one's conscience. The United States is therefore not a nation organized in the service of God, as so often told, but rather a nation designed solely to serve exquisitely individual needs, such as happiness (not excluding love and romance), liberty, the freedoms of speech and press, and religion. The latter, interestingly, is simply one more category on the list of freedoms left to the discretion of the self, with the absence of religion being no less protected than its presence.

The U.S. Constitution (and its surrounding debates and archives) is hardly the first document to glorify the individual self beyond the implications of God and religion. In the sixteenth century—nearly two hundred years before the U.S. Constitution was ratified—the French philosopher Michel de

Montaigne wrote a series of personal essays that were extraordinarily influential, and by no means devoid of God and religion, but nonetheless assert a strong detachment from both. To Montaigne, "Man is a creature indeed obedient to and in the care of God, but which no longer requires God; man is a creature of a nature that has its own power, that forms the single instance of the living of life, and that carries within it an order that no longer relies on grace."[14]

The essays themselves are essentially a form of self-analysis. The topics are random, fragmentary, and often contradictory; their sole purpose, if they indeed have a purpose, is simply to describe the thinking and feeling of Montaigne himself, with the implicit assumption that they are saying something more general about human nature. They are ultimately a testimony to human inner dialogue and an internal frame of reference, which is in sharp contrast to the assumption that all things are predetermined or preordained. Montaigne's essays arguably also represent a substantial change in the perception of human life, evident in due course in the U.S. Constitution (and its related archives) as well. This is particularly true in the elevation of the conscience as the source of "power" that directs human life. Though the conscience is by no means infallible (hence, the necessity of the law), the founders gave it credence by allowing U.S. citizens to make their own choices about religion, firearms, speech, and so forth.

Though the Pilgrims and the Puritans were clearly in the throes of God and religion, Madison and Jefferson more closely resemble the ideal of Montaigne. Madison and Jefferson obviously recognized the value of religion, but nevertheless elevated *internal self-regulation*, and the right to freely think and judge, over all other determinants, religions and governments included. The people, according to the U.S. Constitution, get to decide. God, governments, and monarchs are left out of the loop—certainly where personal discretion exists.

Much of this book will now be devoted to expanding on this argument as it relates to romance in the ivory tower, insisting in particular that above and beyond Ninth Amendment rights, romance and sex should be added to the usual list of First Amendment rights, along with speech, the press, and especially religion. Though this argument is not without limitations, the bottom line is this: the choice of whom to romance, and the right to act on that choice, is no less essential to the formation of the self (and the sphere of personal autonomy) as other well-protected First Amendment rights (e.g., religion, speech, etc.).

Why should romance be added to this First Amendment mix? The answer, ironically, is simple: it shares many similarities to religion. For example, romance is no less relevant to one's *conscience* than religion itself. Romance is also arguably more tempting than religious choices, requiring perhaps more internal debate. Hence, the right to think and judge, based on one's conscience, extends to all matters of substance: speech, the press, religion, and romance, among them.

Finally, though religious organizations are often at the forefront of suppressing sexual rights (and by implication, romantic rights too), they are paradoxically biting the hand that feeds them. Though rarely recognized as such, the First Amendment, at least in spirit, is no less relevant to romance then it is to God. Religion has been safeguarded and thereby protected by the *freedom* to make conscientious choices. That freedom, however, was never limited to religion alone, but instead was extended to all matters of conscience—romance in the ivory tower included. Though as will be demonstrated in the last chapter of this book, romance and sex, and the rights of conscience themselves, found their ultimate home in the Ninth Amendment, the foundation of religious freedom is none other than the liberty of conscience itself.

Before proceeding, one additional constitutional right is worth considering—namely, the right to privacy. Instead of the Ninth Amendment and the rights of conscience, one might alternatively contend that the university, and the government more generally, has no business meddling in the private affairs of professors and students. Romance among consenting adults is clearly a private matter, protected by the right to privacy, no less so than the choices we make about contraception (*Griswold v. Connecticut*) and abortion (*Roe v. Wade*). If this is true, why bother resurrecting First and Ninth Amendment arguments?

Though the right to privacy is a useful vehicle for challenging university prohibitions, it does not explicitly establish an affirmative right for consenting adults to romance. It merely reinforces a specific zone in which the university cannot intrude. While this is certainly progress, and would have the effect of (hopefully) eliminating the prohibitions, it does not in any way or form establish a constitutionally protected privilege for romance among consenting adults.

Here is the heart of the problem. Imagine that the right to privacy was the sole protection for religion; religion per se was not protected but instead privacy rights were invoked to protect religious beliefs and rituals. This, too, may do the trick, at least where government intrusion is concerned, but the right to privacy is not an affirmative right to religious freedom.

Why is this important? An affirmative right that targets a specific class of behaviors (e.g., speech, the press, religion, bearing arms, etc.) creates a much stronger constitutional footing for the presumption of liberty. Privacy, which is simply a barrier against governmental incursion, is substantially different from the freedom of religion. Privacy is ultimately a less persuasive guarantee than the active designation of a specific right. A specific right such as religion signifies a clearly delineated liberty (e.g., religion) immune (in large part) to governmental regulation. This book attempts to delineate a comparable liberty for romantic choice among consenting adults, anchoring it specifically in the rights and liberty of conscience as well as providing First and Ninth Amendment justifications.

Returning to the liberty of conscience, it might be useful at this point to examine the consciences of our ancestors, in particular the intimate affairs of the founders, Jefferson, Madison, Benjamin Franklin, Alexander Hamilton, and Aaron Burr. Compared to romance in the ivory tower, these people made substantially more divisive sexual choices indeed. In fact, their personal lives provide ample testimony to the freedoms afforded to sexual choices, including extramarital affairs, prostitution, pornography, sexual relationships with slaves, contraception, and so on.[15] Their consciences, I infer, were undoubtedly consulted in the service of these choices, no less so than other significant aspects in their lives. Hence, at the very least, protecting the right of consenting adults to make romantic choices is no less consistent with the preferences evident in the lives of the founders.

All of these conclusions are admittedly controversial. Religion provokes controversy, and romance so much more so. Combined, they are at best hostile bedfellows. With this concern in mind, there is the question, How, then, can the present book make its case, with the least amount of damage or offense to the reader? Though the arguments offered herein will not be persuasive to everyone (and furthermore, are conspicuously incomplete), it is still nevertheless crucial to avoid, if possible, offense to all. Perhaps it is best to say that this book ultimately wants to safeguard the right to think and choose, according to one's conscience, as it applies to faculty-student romance, but more important, as it applies in general to the realms of both religion and sexuality. That, essentially, is the goal of this book, which in and of itself is not, at least by premeditation, intended to offend anyone.

Three chapters now follow. The first one examines a prototypical romantic right (i.e., as evidenced in faculty-student romance) relevant to one's *conscience*, and explores the obstacles to recognizing it as such. Romance in the ivory tower is in many respects an ideal issue to examine, since it is truly fundamental to thinking and judging freely. There are perhaps few choices that are as critical as the choice of whom to romance. University prohibitions of such, therefore, are especially pernicious. Moreover, since the ultimate freedom is the ability to make the choice in the first place, a university prohibition that suppresses the choice (in this case, to romance) tramples the very nature of freedom itself.

There is, paradoxically, a long and glorious tradition of using school policies to examine the breadth and vitality of constitutional rights—for example, school prayer (*Abbington School District v. Schempp*), school armband protests (*Tinker v. Des Moines*), sexual material in a school newspaper (*Hazelwood School District v. Kuhlmeier*), and so forth. The venue examined herein is obviously familiar to constitutional scrutiny.

The second chapter takes a broader historical perspective, looking at the precedents underlying both the concepts of liberty and conscience itself. Roger Williams, for instance, is considered at length, as are more contemporary theorists such as John Stuart Mill, Isaiah Berlin, and John Rawls. The relevance of the "right of whom to romance," which underlies the debate about romance in the ivory tower, is explored throughout.

The last chapter examines the U.S. constitutional history of the rights (and liberty) of conscience, Madison's perspective in particular, as well as the historical distinctions between the rights of conscience and religious freedom. Supreme Court cases that are relevant to the liberty of conscience as it relates to sex (e.g., polygamy, as in *Reynolds v. United States*) are discussed too. Most important, the circumstances under which the First Amendment rights of conscience came under Ninth Amendment protection will be proposed and then considered in depth. The ultimate conclusion of this chapter, not surprisingly, is that the liberty of conscience (regardless of where it is located in the Constitution) protects all issues of substance, sex included, but most conspicuously, the choice of whom to romance. This book thereby answers, definitely one hopes, exactly where the power to make romantic choices resides.

1

The Romantic Conscience

Returning to the subject matter of this book, it is useful at this point to briefly define the word conscience. As noted previously, the question underlying the fate of romance in the ivory tower is "where does the power to make the choice reside?" For all intents and purposes, many universities throughout the United States have determined that the power is theirs to wield. This book challenges that assumption, arguing instead that the power is unquestionably within the province of the individual—the aforementioned conscience, in particular. Though generally associated with religion, one's conscience, as indicated earlier, is no less relevant to love and sex as it is to God. Having asserted as much, it is now necessary to turn to the concept of conscience itself, providing both a definition and a historical context for the position defended herein.

The word conscience generally refers to the internal process by which right is distinguished from wrong. This process, not surprisingly, plays an important role in religion, but it is also significant in psychoanalysis as well. What will ultimately concern us here, however, is the manner in which it was used in the letters, drafts, and documents (and so forth) that elevate the role of conscience in both the state and federal constitutions of the United States. Though these writings share a common heritage with religious precedents and utilize the concept of conscience in a manner consistent with psychology (i.e., as the rudder of individual choice), they remain a unique contribution to our understanding of both the U.S. zeitgeist and the foundation of U.S. law.

Thomas Paine's extraordinarily influential pamphlet *Common Sense* is a case in point. Paine declared that the purpose of a constitution is "securing freedom and property to all men, and above all things the free exercise of religion, according to the dictates of conscience."[1] He thereby united conscience and God in what is arguably the earliest (and certainly the most profound) documents promoting a constitutional republic within the United States.

Yet Paine did not mention romance, which is not surprising. *Common Sense* is a treatise on U.S. independence. That notwithstanding, Paine did nonetheless emphasize that governments must facilitate individual freedom and happiness. The latter arguably opens the door for romance (or more generally, sexual rights), since it is hard to imagine individual freedom and happiness without it.

Though the word conscience has now been defined, and its importance to Paine demonstrated, the question still remains, What, exactly, did the term conscience mean to the architects of the U.S. Constitution? Was it ever carefully defined therein? Although it was paired with religious liberty, could it be relevant to other liberties as well? Love, sex, and romance, for example? Madison's comments are particularly instructive for gaining insight into and perhaps resolving this first issue.

Madison, curiously, distinguished two types of conscience. The first and more familiar is that conscience, like reason, is derived from God, the ultimate source of all things human. There is, however, a second position, which is more relevant to the discussion herein. Namely, that Madison also elevated conscience as the source of inalienable rights—in particular, the rights to think, choose, and judge. As Adrienne Koch noted, "The recognition of the unalienability of man's right to think and choose and judge is at the heart of [Madison's] theory."[2]

Conscience, in this latter formulation, is divorced from religious doctrine. In fact, it supersedes it. The inalienable rights of conscience permit the U.S. populace to think, choose, and judge *without* the constraints of religious proscriptions in general, or a national religion in particular. Religious texts are therefore neither required nor in essence needed to dictate the actions of U.S. citizens. They are entitled to think on their own, having the freedom to draw from a wide range of influential sources, including political theory, philosophy, moral sentiments, ethics, the Bible, and so forth.

If religion was never meant to monopolize the process of conscience in the United States, what is its putative role? It is, as stated previously, the handmaiden to the rights derived from conscience itself.

So, for example, presume that a married couple is trying to decide whether to have children. If we take the perspective of the founders, Madison in particular, this couple should let their respective (and collective) conscience be their guide. They should decide what they think is right, and prepare themselves for the consequences. Biblical proclamations or admonishments are relevant if, *and only if*, the couple *chooses* to make them such. It is the choice, derived from one's conscience, that elevates the role of religion and not, as usually presumed, the other way around.

The significant point is this: when it comes to the choices we make, it is the choice *itself* that represents the right and thereby sets the ground rules, not a religious text pontificating on such. Pundits, religious or otherwise (universities included), can repeatedly expound on the rules and requirements for behaving. These opinions, however, are secondary to the privilege of making the choice itself. It is ultimately the choice that is the constitutionally protected right—whether our beliefs in God or who we romance (and how we act on it)—university proclamations notwithstanding.

Protection is a word worth emphasizing. It is common, for example, to conclude that rights emanate from the Constitution itself. This is a reasonable assumption, since the Constitution makes explicit statements about them. Reasonable or not, though, it is ultimately wrong. It is comparable to concluding that museums create art, because art is displayed in museums. Though it is true that our rights are described in the Constitution, our rights themselves preexist it. In fact, they preexist all constitutions and governments. This belief is evident in the work of Paine, Madison, Jefferson, and many others. These authors concluded that natural rights, like nature itself, are provided for the benefit of humanity. Governments and constitutions, in contrast, are given power solely to protect the public welfare and individual natural rights—that is, *all* natural rights, despite prejudices to the contrary.

Romance and Sex on a College Campus

Turning again to the topics of romance and sex, it is now useful to more fully examine romance in the ivory tower as it relates to the dictates of conscience. Marriage prohibitions will not be the focal point of the present chapter, which instead stresses the antecedent right of choosing whom to romance.

The present chapter therefore intends to examine a specific prohibition to romance (among faculty and students) and its various manifestations.

Though romance among consenting adults is not usually proscribed in the United States, except as previously mentioned among psychotherapists and their clients, there is in fact at least one other venue in which romance is occasionally prohibited: the workplace environment. A romantic relationship among coworkers can be grounds for dismissal. While obviously not criminalized, a workplace romance that results in the loss of a job is no less impacting, certainly financially, than equivalent forms of criminal sanctions (e.g., fines, probation, etc.). It is thus perhaps no less insidious than other romantic prohibitions, thereby making it a suitable topic for introducing the discussion here.

Recent surveys indicate that 58 percent of employees have been involved in an office romance.[3] Love apparently makes the world go around, even while we work. Perhaps this should come as no surprise. Americans spend more and more time at work, and in doing so, they share responsibilities, proximity, values, and so forth, making romance an inevitable consequence of the workplace environment.

Some have suggested that the workplace is especially ideal for mate selection because the repeated exposure and performance observations are better sources of information about a perspective partner than the information gleaned from a date or pickup at a bar or club.

Although U.S. workers are romantically inclined, their bosses are not necessarily happy with this situation. A 2005 poll of human resource professionals (conducted by the *Wall Street Journal* in conjunction with the Society of Human

Resources Management) indicated that approximately 18 percent of the firms surveyed had a written policy addressing workplace romance.[4] Various strategies were evident, ranging from strict prohibitions of romantic involvement to negative performance reviews when romance was detected. These policies, called "nonfraternization," were either written, as indicated above, or simply verbal (and thereby told to employees). Implicit (and unstated) corporate policies were also evident, such as the colloquial, "Do not fish from the company pier."

Why, you may wonder, do companies prohibit romance in the first place? Is it from a concern with productivity? Or is it something more personal, such as an aversion to romance itself?

Both beliefs undoubtedly play some part in these prohibitions. But the truth of the matter is that the primary motivation for the nonfraternization policy is the belief that it reduces civil liability in sexual harassment lawsuits.[5] That, ultimately, is the bottom line of why coworkers cannot fraternize.

It is also, incidentally, the same reason why professors and students cannot fraternize (or romance), the rhetoric about power differentials and favoritism notwithstanding. Universities have banned consensual relationships because like their corporate counterparts, they too believe that it will reduce their civil liability in sexual harassment lawsuits.[6]

How, you may wonder, can this be true? Or more specifically, what does romance among consenting adults have to do with sexual harassment?

The real answer is precisely nothing. Romance, by definition, is desired and consensual. Sexual harassment is exactly the opposite: unwanted and coerced. The big question, then, is why should consensual romance be denied in the service of protecting against sexual harassment lawsuits?

Here is how it works. Title IX of the Education Amendments of 1972 asserts that "no person in the United States shall, on the basis of sex, be excluded from participation in, be denied the benefits of, or should be subject to discrimination under any education program or activity receiving Federal financial assistance."[7]

What does this have to do with sexual harassment? It is as follows: the Supreme Court, in *Franklin v. Gwinnet County Public Schools,* concluded that the sexual harassment of a student by a teacher is a form of sex discrimination under Title IX because it corrupts the educational environment and diminishes academic benefits.

How is sexual harassment defined in this situation? Educational institutions, including universities, have generally followed the guidelines issued by the Economic Employment Opportunity Commission pursuant to Title VII of the Civil Rights Act, which was designed to provide protection against sexual harassment in the workplace.[8] Two types of sexual harassment were identified. The first is usually called the "quid pro quo," whereby an unwanted sexual contact is made mandatory for employment or an employment-related decision (e.g., promotion).

The second type of sexual harassment is generally defined as the "hostile environment," whereby sexual innuendos, behaviors, or symbols are used to create an intimidating, hostile, or offensive workplace atmosphere. Companies, not surprisingly, are potentially liable if they permit or ignore either of these forms of sexual harassment. (See, for example, the cases of *Faragher v. City of Boca Raton, Burlington, Ind., Inc. v. Ellerth*, and *Pennsylvania State Police v. Suders.*)

Other nuances of sexual harassment law exist as well. For example, even if an employee engaged in a sexual relationship with a supervisor, the employee may still have an actionable civil lawsuit if they felt compelled to engage in sex in order to preserve their job (see *Meritor Savings Bank v. Vinson*). Even more complicated is the field of third-party civil lawsuits, whereby, for instance, nonromancing employees can claim harm or disadvantage in comparison to romancing employees. This could occur if a supervisor provides privileges and promotions to their lover(s), but withholds similar benefits from other equally qualified (or even better qualified) nonlover employees (see *Miller et al. v. Department of Corrections et al.*).

Still, even if each of these examples provides a credible rationale for a sexual harassment lawsuit, they are nevertheless a far cry from a desired and mutually consensual romance. What, then, is the tie that binds them?

It is simply this. Imagine that two employees, a male and a female, fall madly in love. Or alternatively, imagine that a male professor and a female student fall madly in love as well. Bliss, in either case, is the end result. But lo and behold, after nine months the relationship goes awry, imploding shortly thereafter.

At this point, the female wants out and demands no further personal contact with the male. The male, however, starts pestering the female. He wants another chance. When this doesn't work, he becomes hostile. As his hostility escalates, the female feels harassed.

Guess what? She files a sexual harassment complaint and thereafter a civil lawsuit.

Whether this actually happens or not is immaterial. Companies and universities assert (at least privately) that the potential exists, and as such, sweep consensual dating into their sexual harassment policies, with civil rights being damned.

Is this fair? Or more important, is this legal?

It is of course patently unfair. The only real question is whether it is legal, or more significantly, treated as legal.

Two factors warrant mention. The first is the opinion of Catharine MacKinnon, a prominent "radical" (or arguably, "antisex") feminist legal scholar. MacKinnon has asserted that all romantic relationships in the workplace (even those that culminate in marriage) are sexual harassment. Men, she argues, dominate and control women so thoroughly in the workplace that it is impossible for women to mutually consent to romance.[9] (MacKinnon, incidentally, has also proclaimed that pornography is the rape of an actress, because pornographic actresses, like women in the workplace, are incapable of giving consent to sex.)[10]

Though it is easy to dismiss MacKinnon's perspective as sheer nonsense, plus demeaning (and insulting) to both men and women, the fact of the matter is that her opinions were persuasive, at least in the 1980s and early 1990s. Which may also account for the second factor worth mentioning: namely, that a number of courts, during this same time period, upheld private employer rights to enforce nonfraternization policies (*Patton v. J. C. Penney*, *Sarsha v. Sears Roebuck & Co.*, and *Rogers v. International Business Machines Co.*).

Fortunately, this circumstance has changed recently, whereby states (e.g., California) are now enacting statutory law protecting employees against invasion of privacy by their employers. Feminist legal scholarship has also shifted, whereby women's personal autonomy and agency is recognized and facilitated.[11]

Where does this leave us now? Despite the slur on romance in the workplace, such prohibitions are by no means universal in corporate America. Some companies welcome romance among their employees. Ben & Jerry's Ice Cream, for instance, has gone on record stating, "We expect that our employees will date, fall in love, and become partners. If a problem comes up, we encourage employees to let us know and we'll talk about it."[12]

Even more striking is the position of Southwest Airlines (which has been rated by *Fortune* magazine as being in the top five of the "Best Companies to Work for in America"): "A happy employee" Southwest asserts, "is a productive employee," noting that it has 2,200 staff members whose spouses also work for the company.[13]

Returning now to faculty-student romance, it might be useful to ask what can be learned from corporate America? A lot it turns out. First, where sanctions exist, the university and corporate worlds both have much in common. Romance can lead to the termination of employment. The basic constitutional issue, interestingly, is also decidedly the same. It boils down to the question of whether the choice of whom to romance is a constitutionally protected right (like conscience, for example) that supersedes the designs (e.g., to reduce civil liability) and etiquette of employers/universities, or whether it is among the various characteristics (such as a dress code) or reasons (e.g., will adversely affect the company) that can be regulated according to employer/university discretion.

Although corporate America is on a stronger footing here, particularly where corporate disadvantage is concerned, the university must instead persuade its constituency that it has legitimate reasons for prohibiting romance in the first place, without further acknowledging the benefits it derives from these prohibitions in sexual harassment lawsuits. These prohibitions are not legal either, but the university and its employees now treat them as such. This book will hopefully reverse this situation.

The Drama of It All

A romantic relationship between a professor and a student has obvious dramatic appeal, having been portrayed in both novels and movies. The curious part, however, is that its real-life counterpart may soon be extinct. Since university prohibitions pit constitutionally protected romantic rights against the power of institutional policy, they represent, in many respects, a classic duel between the rights of the people and governmental powers. The ultimate question to keep in mind as we proceed is this: Does the liberty (or rights) of conscience protect the choice of whom to romance as much as the choice of what to believe in?

This question, incidentally, is not much different in principle than the question of whether the First Amendment's freedom of speech protects sex as much as politics. The answer is yes, but not always. It can protect pornography, but not if it is deemed obscene (*Miller v. California*). It can protect Larry Flynt (of *Hustler* magazine fame) when he publishes a parody of Reverend Jerry Falwell (implying that Falwell had sex with his mother in an outhouse [*Hustler Magazine Inc. v. Falwell*]), but not protect Darlene Miller when dancing nude in Indiana at the Kitty Kat Lounge (*Barnes v. Glen Theatre, Inc*). Many other examples would suffice as well, but the conclusion remains the same. Yes, speech protects sex, but not in its entirety. Presumably, if the arguments presented here are persuasive, the same finding will eventually prevail for the rights of conscience. Romance among consenting adults is protected, but not completely. Exceptions will undoubtedly arise as well.

Two final points are worth considering before delving more deeply into professor-student romance. First, are the rights of conscience *natural rights*? Meaning, simply, are they rights that are integral to the nature of humanity? And if so, what is the relationship between the rights and *liberty* of conscience?

As noted previously, Madison clearly designated the rights of conscience as natural rights when he described them as *inalienable*. Inalienable, by definition, asserts that a right is undeniably instrumental to humankind and fully protected by the law. The liberty of conscience is similar. It, too, is an inalienable right. It is generally used to refer to the *exercise* of the rights of conscience, in the form of having the right to make deliberations that rely on one's conscience.

So to summarize, both the rights and liberty of conscience are basic to the needs of human nature, and therefore cannot be denied or indiscriminately abridged by governments (and most certainly, quasi-governing bodies such as universities). The additional distinction of the liberty of conscience is simply to further recognize the very *process* by which the individual asserts their own individuality in the choices one makes about matters that are deeply relevant to one's well-being. Religion is the obvious example of such, but as this book also maintains, it is by no means the only choice that comes under the process of conscientious scrutiny. Whom to romance, as repeatedly noted, is equally relevant to such deliberations.

All You Need Is Love

"Love conquers all things," noted Virgil in the first century BC, "let us too surrender to Love."

This is no doubt a fine sentiment, unless, as previously elaborated, it is in reference to romance between a professor and their student. In that case, the following is more apropos: If you lose your heart, you could lose your job.

Take, for example, the University of Wisconsin at Madison policy on consensual relationships (included in its sexual harassment guidelines), which warns that

the university presumes that the ability to make objective decisions is compromised if there is a romantic and/or sexual relationship between two individuals who have a reporting or evaluative relationship. There is almost always a power differential between such individuals that not only obscures objectivity but also influences perceptions of consensuality. The individual with the power or status advantage is required by university policy to report the relationship to his or her supervisor and will be accountable for failing to make this report.[14]

Or for yet another example, consider Yale University's policy on consensual relationships:

The integrity of the teacher-student relationship is the foundation of the University's educational mission. This relationship vests considerable trust in the teacher, whom, in turn, bear authority and accountability as a mentor, educator, and evaluator. The unequal institutional power inherent in this relationship heightens the vulnerability of the student and the potential for coercion. The pedagogical relationship between teacher and student must be protected from influences or activities that can interfere with learning consistent with the goals and ideals of the University. Whenever a teacher is responsible for directly supervising a student, a sexual relationship between them is inappropriate. Any such relationship jeopardizes the integrity of the educational process by creating a conflict of interest and may lead to an inhospitable learning environment for other students. Therefore, no teacher shall have a sexual relationship with a student over whom he or she has direct supervisory responsibilities regardless of whether the relationship is consensual. Teachers must avoid sexual relationships with their students, including those for whom they are likely to have future supervisory responsibility. Conversely, teachers must not directly supervise any student with whom they have a sexual relationship. Violations of or the failure to correct violations of these conflict of interest principles by the teacher will be grounds for disciplinary action.[15]

Both of these universities, and many others like them, have obviously concluded that the power differential and the prospect of evaluation are sufficient enough to offset any constitutional claims to preserve the right to romance among consenting adults. The consensual relationship policies are clear testimony to this fact.

Here, however, is the curious part. No mention is ever made of an alternative remedy, such as third-party evaluation, that would preserve the right to romance. Far worse, then again, is the fact that all of these consensual relationship policies fail to acknowledge that they were instituted in large part to reduce civil liability in sexual harassment litigation. This omission, in particular, is especially hypocritical. It is ultimately a failure to disclose a conflict of interest—that is, that the policies have a litigation benefit to the university over and above the rhetoric about power. In this respect, it is no different from a medical researcher who fails to disclose funding by a drug company. It also raises the same suspicions about reported findings (e.g., power, favoritism, etc.). The paradox in all of this, incidentally, is that a professor is required to confess and pay the price for a consensual romantic entanglement with a student, whereas a university need not confess its motivation about saving money.

Retained by the People

Returning once again to the basic constitutional issues, it is readily apparent that these policies ignore Ninth Amendment constitutional rights. This is not surprising, since such rights are routinely ignored elsewhere as well. Nevertheless, when the Ninth Amendment is examined ("The enumeration in the

Constitution, of certain rights, shall not be construed to deny or disparage others retained by the people") it seems difficult to avoid the conclusion that the word "others" would not have application to the choices consenting adults make about romance. If, as often proclaimed, "love makes the world go round," it must at the very least be protected by the Ninth Amendment.[16]

Of greater concern is the presumption that a university has a legitimate interest in regulating the intimate lives of its faculty. Though certainly not as extreme as censoring books read on campus, or perhaps a required campus diet, these policies nonetheless represent a perverse corruption of university power. If the church is separated from the state, the university, it would seem, should be no less separate from the intimate lives of its faculty—the choice of romance being no less governed by the rights and liberty of conscience than other intimate choices of substance too.

If this is true, how have these prohibitions survived? The answer, apparently, is that they survive on the coattails of moral indignation. That is, the policies prohibiting romance between faculty and students capitalize on vague notions of romantic impropriety. The implications of such impropriety, as noted in the policies quoted above, is by no means limited to faculty-student romance, but has been instrumental to most sex-related prohibitions (including film, literature, advertising, performance, sodomy, etc.) in the United States. Many of these have fortunately now been overturned.

Furthermore, the truth of the matter is that the freedom to romance is no less fraught with difficult outcomes than the freedom of speech. Both are protected in spite of this circumstance, however, because liberty depends on it. Thus, if impropriety exists, it is no less evident in the university when it prohibits romance than it is in the intimacy between faculty and students.

Here is another perspective to consider. Imagine instead that religious practices or perhaps prayer were prohibited on campus—as in, if you pray on campus, you could lose your job. Outrage would no doubt result. A Supreme Court justice or two would condemn it, and the president as well. The media would most certainly also join in the fray, offended in a morally righteous kind of way by this insolence.

There are, of course, many differences between religion and romance. Notably, one is spiritual, and the other is corporeal. Neither, however, is necessarily void of both. These differences notwithstanding, it is important from a constitutional point of view to highlight their similarities, at least where the operations of conscience are concerned.

Both, for example, are intimate and highly cherished. They also both go to the heart of personal autonomy. Both serve as the foundation for self-identity as well. Finally, both are extraordinarily consuming. People give their "heart and soul" to romance and religion.

If they have similarities, why do colleges discriminate against one but not the other? The answer, of course, is obvious. Religion has enormous power and influence, often unparalleled in the United States. Romance between a professor and a student can hardly hope to compete. Yet it is nevertheless a disgrace, I believe, for an institution, particularly a university, ostensibly dedicated to high ideals, to minimize the rights of conscience by precluding consenting adults from choosing, thinking, and judging whom to romance.

If this is true, the question, then, is what to do about it? Rescinding the policy at universities and colleges throughout the United States is an obvious solution. What will it take to achieve this goal? In my view, it is the creation of a constitutional foundation for making fundamental life choices, whereby romance is no less sacred than religion. The key, as mentioned repeatedly, is the rights and liberty of conscience.

University of California, the Avenger

To illustrate this issue more fully, the University of California policy prohibiting faculty-student romance will now be examined. Though there are certainly more egregious policies in existence (Ohio Northern University, for example, bans all sexual contact between professors and students, except when married), the primary objective is simply to demonstrate, using the University of California policy as an example, that romance and sex are significant representatives of an essential civil liberty falling under the discretion of one's conscience.

Let us begin with the question of how the University of California romance policy came into existence.

It started, lo and behold, with a case of sexual assault. The backstory, apparently, is that a prominent male professor at the University of California at Berkeley got drunk and sexually assaulted a female student. The entire University of California system (which includes UCLA) thereafter moved to prohibit consensual sex and romance between faculty and the students they teach or oversee.

This policy is based, as suggested previously, on the assumption that sex invites abuse; or that by prohibiting the former, it will eliminate the later. The resultant University of California policy, approved by the Assembly of the Academic Senate on May 28, 2003, and adopted by the Board of Regents on July 17, 2003, states the following: "The revised policy prohibits a faculty member from entering into a romantic or sexual relationship with any student for whom that faculty member currently has or prospectively might have academic responsibility."[17]

Some readers, without question, will hail this policy as long overdue, arguing that the job of a professor is to teach, and the job of the student is to learn. Everything else is inappropriate or superfluous. Similarly, as noted previously, readers who have concerns with the power differential between professors and students, and the potential for favoritism, will perhaps consider this policy wise as well. (These sentiments are undoubtedly also shared by those who supported this change in policy.)

Not everyone, of course, was enamored with this change. Some were outright offended by it, believing instead that it is an unconscionable encroachment on the individual rights of professors and students alike.

Curiously, despite the difference of opinions, there was no protest movement precipitated by the change. There were no professor-student love-ins, for example, on the UCLA campus—my commentary in the *Los Angeles Times* being perhaps one of the only public murmurs.[18]

It is admittedly a difficult position to advocate. As my correspondence with the *Los Angeles Times* clearly demonstrated, one's motives are questioned; and it could potentially be a political liability as well (certainly if one is seeking higher office). On the other hand, I believe it is an *ideal* right to advocate because it does not discriminate by race, creed, national origin, or sexual orientation. All professors and students come under its jurisdiction. In this circumstance, it is democratic, which in many respects is what makes it so unusual. Here, perhaps, is another way of looking at this.

Imagine this scenario instead. A prominent professor, female this time, has $100 in her purse. She is robbed on the UCLA campus. In response, the university proclaims "no more money (or purses) on campus," thereby equating the availability of money with precipitating the crime of robbery.

Outrage would no doubt result. Without money, faculty could not buy books on campus, thereby eliminating a cherished liberty. Why not, faculty might assert, hire more campus police and hence reduce the crime of robbery? It would seem more appropriate than punishing faculty for carrying cash.

The same argument could be made about romance. Why equate it with precipitating the crimes of rape or sexual harassment? Tackling the crime itself is always more efficacious than eliminating an essential liberty. Why, I might ask, is romance punished when a drunken professor commits a crime?

Taking this a step further, I could also ask, Where would this end? Again, using the example of prohibiting money on campus, one could contend that its absence would provoke criminals to target other assets, such as laptop computers. Would the university thereafter prohibit laptops? And what about books, which can be stolen as well? Obviously, at some point the university, in order to continue operating, would have to stop prohibiting things that can be abused or stolen, and instead turn its attention to stopping the crime itself.

Which brings the discussion back to romance. Does the University of California (or any other college or university) need a policy prohibiting romance among consenting adults to prevent abuses? This is a reasonable question, and the answer would be affirmative, if one condition was met. Namely, if relevant state statutes did not criminalize such abuses in the first place, universities would need to develop their own criteria for defining sexual abuses and their corresponding punishments.

As is well-known, however, sexual abuses (e.g., rape, sexual assault, sexual molestation, etc.), in contrast to "power abuses" or "status abuses" (e.g., not crediting junior colleagues with authorship), are consistently criminalized. For example, California criminal statutes governing the absence of informed consent in sexual matters apply equally to all members of the university community. The same point is true about sexual harassment. Workplace laws—which allow for criminal and civil remedies relating to hostile environments and quid pro quo—already cover such conduct on college campuses. Thus, there is no need for university policies prohibiting sexual abuses, as there is no need for university policies prohibiting armed robbery or murder. All such crimes are illegal, regardless of where they are performed.

If the University of California (or other universities and colleges in the United States) does not need a policy prohibiting sexual abuse, why would it censor sex and romance among faculty and students? There is, as noted previously, the legitimate concerns with power differences and favoritism. Though certainly valid objections, they are hardly unique to romance, and are by no means sufficiently destructive enough to offset protecting the rights to think, choose, and judge.

The real reason for these prohibitions, as I (and others) asserted earlier, is that universities want to further reduce their liability in civil lawsuits—no sex and romance means no negligence. This strategy is feasible, perhaps even desirable, in the circumstance where the liberty of conscience is narrowly defined, and where sexual rights (such as the choice of whom to romance) are not fully recognized and securely protected.

Employers, for obvious reasons, want to distance themselves (and be held blameless) from the egregious behavior of employees. For example, if an employee harms someone (or commits a crime) while at work, the employer is highly moti-vated to establish independence (hence, no responsibility) for such acts as a means of reducing the potential for employer liability and negligence. Hospitals, police departments, dance studios, and so forth, are instances of employers that in civil lawsuits have attempted to distance themselves from the harms created by their employees. Sometimes they are successful, and at other times they are not.

Yet where sexual harassment (or abuse) is concerned, the courts, in civil lawsuits, have generally recognized employer in-dependence (i.e., the absence of culpability) if one condition is met: if prior to the sexually harassing incident, the employer had established and distributed a policy that defines and attempts to prevent sexual harassment itself (plus vigorously investigates and resolves such complaints). If the latter is true, an employer is generally no longer held liable for an employ-ee's act of sexual harassment. Hence, the plaintiff (the person harmed) can only sue the employee, not the employer. There are exceptions, but they tend to be limited to negligent hiring and supervision—that is, cases in which the employer hired an employee with a known history of sexual harassment, or the employer failed to act on knowledge of a current sexually ha-rassing situation.

One additional exception also deserves mention. An em-ployer who merely circulates an e-mail about sexual ha-rassment, which employees quickly delete, will have great difficulty establishing in a court of law that a reasonable effort was made to prevent sexual harassment. Consequently, employers who are serious about reducing their liability to sex-ual harassment lawsuits usually institute policies and practices that are more consistent with an attempt to eliminate the be-havior itself. Large companies, or universities in particular, tend to be highly motivated to put these policies in place for the twofold purpose of limiting financial damages and ensuring a more harmonious workplace. Thus, hiring sexual harassment personnel, running sexual harassment seminars, creating a sexual harassment manual, and so forth, are the types of interventions commonly utilized by such employers.

Recently, as cited earlier, a new twist has been added, particularly at universities and other large corporations: eliminating sex and romance itself. As noted above, this is based on the assumption that this policy will further reduce the probability that the employer will be held responsible for the harm created by a sexually harassing (or abusing) employee. Thus, despite the rhetoric about drunken male professors or the quality of the educational environment, the real reason for this policy at UCLA and elsewhere, I (and others) assert, is that it helps save money. And in this respect, it is no different from many other decisions on college campuses, be it the use of temporary instructors, the unionizing of graduate students, or the operation of the physical plant. Cost is always critical.

The big question, however, is what college professors and students are *paying* in terms of their liberties to potentially save the university money in civil litigation.[19]

It needs to be emphasized at the outset that there is nothing wrong with saving money. The university's goal of limiting civil liability is also understandable and certainly warranted, particularly in light of our litigious society. What is problematic, though, is the strategy itself. One needs to question whether an alternative would suffice—that is, a tactic that reduced the university's vulnerability in civil litigation, but did not violate the constitutional rights of its faculty and students.

Here is another way of looking at this that relates directly to sex. A rape by a male professor of a female undergraduate occurs in the evening in a darkened parking lot on a university campus. A civil lawsuit results from this crime, and the victim (or plaintiff) is successful in her effort to hold the university partly responsible. What does the university, in this circumstance, do to protect itself in the future? Does it eliminate cars from campus? Or prohibit the use of parking lots? Or perhaps exclude professors from them? Certainly not; instead, it adds sufficient lighting to parking lots, increases the police force, institutes a campus escort service to parking lots, and so forth, thereby ensuring the reduction of the crime without eliminating liberties from the rest of the college campus. The same is arguably necessary when separating crime from romance.

As underscored earlier, the constitutional archives demonstrate that U.S. citizens have a fundamental right to make choices based on their conscience about essential affiliations, notably religion, but also by implication, friends, professional associations, political parties, and sexual or romantic partners. Choosing a romantic partner, in particular, is a basic right unquestionably anchored in the Ninth Amendment, which as noted above recognizes rights "retained by the people," independent of state or government intervention.[20] It is unquestionably a Ninth Amendment right because U.S. citizens (at least white heterosexuals) have rarely allowed the government, be it state or federal, to tell consenting adults whom they can romance (with the obvious exception, for instance, of a psychotherapist and their client). Such measures, if they do exist, appear in futuristic fiction like *Brave New World* or religious prohibitions such as marrying someone outside the faith. It was for this very reason that our country does not have a national religion. We are guaranteed the right to think, choose, and judge based on our own conscience alone, if we prefer it.

Even more important, our constitutional history and the U.S. Supreme Court as well demand a compelling reason for any curtailment of our constitutional rights—war, for example. Reducing negligence in a sexual harassment lawsuit hardly fits the bill. Moreover, any legitimate limitation on our constitutional rights must be implemented in the least restrictive manner possible. Prohibiting sexual and romantic relationships on the off chance that they might go awry and result in a civil lawsuit against the university amounts to, once again, "burning down the house to roast the pig." Or to put it another way, destroying everything to achieve a specific goal, when a simple solution would have sufficed (e.g., third-party evaluation).

As an alternative, for example, the University of California (or any other college or university so inclined) could require all the faculty and students to read and sign a *release* (sometimes called a "Love Contract") warning them about the potential problems with dating between faculty and students— the inherent power differential, the appearance of favoritism, etc. By signing, these faculty and students would be acknowledging that they understand the risks, and that they promise to hold the university blameless if a romantic relationship develops and thereafter goes awry.

So warned, daters could proceed at their own risk. If romantic malfeasance occurred, the university would have a document (and a policy) in place to limit its civil liability. The Love Contract would function much like the release that patients are required to sign before undergoing a major medical procedure. Though such releases are by no means a guarantee of protection in civil litigation, warning statements are nevertheless useful in civil lawsuits. (It should also be noted that having a policy that prohibits faculty-student romance does not guarantee protection in civil litigation as well, particularly where negligent supervision claims are concerned.)

Another alternative to the prohibition of consensual relationships is called the "nexus principle." It is drawn from labor arbitration case law and concerns itself with the regulation of employee off-duty conduct. According to this principle, a university could regulate consensual romantic relationships, but only if it demonstrated with specific facts that the conduct adversely impacted the operation of the university itself.

What would it take to convince an arbitrator? For example, it would mean demonstrating that the romance damaged a university's reputation or interfered with its ability to teach. It should be noted, however, that arbitrators have consistently held that an employer cannot interfere with the private life of an employee, unless it can prove that the employee's conduct adversely effected business interests in a relevant manner.[21]

Finally, although Hollywood is fond of depicting love affairs between aging male professors and young female undergraduates, such fairy tales surely are the exception rather than the norm. A much more plausible scenario imagines a thirty-something professor and a twenty-something graduate student who work together and fall in love. Matrimony is a much more likely outcome than a civil lawsuit. This is particularly true, given the numbers. There are well over a half million graduate students (masters programs, PhD programs, law schools, medical schools, etc.) in the United States alone. Their number, feelings, and choices are by no means trivial.

It is easy, of course, to be offended or even outraged by the image of a sleazy male college professor. That notwithstanding, it is important to emphasize that the trait of sleaziness is not prohibited in university romance policies (nor even defined, for that matter), despite the discomfort it engenders, in large part because such behavior is more subtle (e.g., standing too close to a student, leering glares, etc.) but impacting nonetheless.

In contrast, sex and romance rarely, if ever, actually occur in the classroom. Yet as it now stands, those faculty and students who truly fall in love are the ones whose rights of conscience, I believe, are being infringed and thereby unduly punished, while their leering (but nondating) colleagues are left to their own devices.

If university romance policies are constitutionally unjust, the next step is to ask whether this is something worth fighting over. There are, of course, many injustices in the world. Is romance in the ivory tower among them? One could maintain that sex and romance are hardly cherished liberties when compared to the freedoms of speech and the press. For instance, it could be alleged that students and faculty have other options, such as dropping out of classes or graduate programs, to pursue their romantic and sexual interests. This is certainly true, but it sounds suspiciously like the underlying dynamic in "separate but equal"—that is, go elsewhere. Universities, even nondenominational ones, would not banish faculty and students who chose to pray together in their private lives—a behavior that arguably also creates intimate bonds, and could lead to favoritism, questions of coercion (if it represents a change in a student's religious faith), and so forth.

Enforcement is another issue. If couples are discrete, who will catch them? Similarly, might others be disinclined to report offenses should they or their friends fall in love as well? This is perhaps another good reason to avoid such policies in the first place.

There is also the issue raised above of whether sex and romance, the liberty of conscience notwithstanding, belong in the classroom itself. On the face it, the obvious answer would be no, and as such, might this prohibition serve a higher educational mission that should be supported? This belief, which is sincere and held by some members of the academic community, fails to appreciate that the real institutional motive for the policy is not, I believe, problems with classroom instruction but instead, as I have repeatedly stated, civil liability. The question is therefore whether it is appropriate or even necessary to trade civil liberties for decreased liability in civil litigation.

Furthermore, the belief that a prohibition on faculty-student romance will enhance instruction is itself misguided as well as disingenuous. These policies have not now, nor have they ever been, about sex and romance in the classroom. The classroom, the office, or the department is merely the place where faculty and students interact (i.e., the workplace environment). If romance and sex follow, it is obviously expressed *in private*, much like our religious beliefs and practices. Both are inappropriate in the classroom, and thereby contrary to an educational mission when expressed therein.

On the other hand, when romance or prayer exists in one's private life (among consenting adults) an entirely different issue is at stake. Namely, the ways in which we pray or romance are fundamental to the conscientious choices we make about our personal lives. They often represent the core of self-identity as it relates to religion and family. This point, as noted previously, is the leitmotif of this book. Taking this even a step further, this book suggests that the concepts of choice and conscience are among the primary philosophical principles underlying the U.S. Constitution, equally relevant to the spirit as well as the flesh.

It is also important to stress that the belief that romance curtails an educational mission trades on the stereotype of the lecherous male professor seducing gullible female undergraduates. Though lecherous male professors undoubtedly exist, the big question, implied earlier, is whether they are a sufficient enough reason to prohibit romance for everyone else.

Here is another curious point. Despite the rhetoric about faculty-student romance, seduction on a college campus occurs primarily among the students themselves. This is particularly true of flirting. Professors, by and large, are teaching. Distracted students are another matter. One could claim, purely for the sake of argument, that flirting students (making "eyes" at each other) are interfering with nonflirting students, thereby thwarting the teaching process as well, but like other expressions of romance, this is perhaps best left to the discretion of those involved, unless it is truly disruptive, whereby it need not be prohibited but deferred instead—outside the classroom, for example.

Furthermore, in those cases where teacher-student romance truly exists, it is much more likely to occur between a graduate student, working as a teaching assistant, who falls in love with an undergraduate student, than between professors and undergraduates. The age difference is minimal, interests are likely to be similar, and it is much more probable that mutual attractions would occur. These characteristics are essential to sex and romance, and are surprising to no one.

It is also crucial to ask, What is the probability that an eighteen- to twenty-one-year-old undergraduate is attracted to and shares similar interests with a forty-year-old (or beyond) professor (be it male or female), so much so that sex and romance is pursued? One presumes that this probability is small.

Forty-year-old professors or their older colleagues are more likely to evoke images of mom or dad, or even grandpa or grandma, among many undergraduate students. Though these concerns are obviously irrelevant to protecting the liberty of conscience, they are being raised here to address the question of whether this is truly a problem in the first place. Clearly, there are professors who abuse their roles in the course of their employment. This is equally true, however, of police officers, lawyers, judges, members of Congress, and so on. Eliminating civil liberties to punish a small number of transgressors is hardly the answer.

That notwithstanding, it is still undoubtedly useful to get objective data (using representative national samples) on faculty-student romance for the simple purpose of obtaining answers to critical questions. For instance, as a starting point, how many undergraduate women have had romantic or sexual relationships with male professors? What is the percentage, 1 or 5 percent? And of that percentage, what percent regret those relationships? (Or in general, how would they evaluate the quality of the relationship?) The answer to this question alone is critical to whether this should be framed as problematic in the first place. Similarly, it is also important to assess the age of the parties involved, the duration of the relationships, the sexual orientation of both parties, and other relevant demographics, like class size, student enrollment, geographic location, marital status, religious affiliation (of the parties and the college), and so on. Finally, it is also essential to include "control" questions, such as the quality of teaching. One may discover that poor teaching is a more pronounced problem than faculty-student romance gone awry. If so, perhaps the quality of teaching is a better focus for university resources and policies than matchmaking on campus.

The percentage of female undergraduates who have romanced male professors is also irrelevant to the liberties of graduate students, who may wish to romance professors, and the liberties of professors themselves, who obviously have constitutional rights, I believe, to date consenting adults of their choice. Thus, this issue ultimately comes down to *whose* choice is most important: faculty and students making conscientious choices about whom to romance, or universities exercising their "power" to infringe on such choices?

The answer should be patently obvious: that the choice to romance is much more important as a constitutional foundation than the university's right to preclude it. As repeatedly asserted throughout this book, the choices that consenting adults make about romance are no less fundamental than the choices adults make about their beliefs in God (and both, I emphasize, precipitate relevant actions, either romantic or religious in nature). Since the latter was instrumental in the founding of both the nation and the Constitution, it behooves us to protect the former with the same persistence and rigor as the latter.

Which raises another question. If sex and romance were both fundamental life choices made by U.S. citizens, and arguably protected by the First and Ninth Amendments, why would a university trample them in the service of saving money? One problem is the lack of recognition of these particular First and Ninth Amendment rights themselves. It is probably easier to ignore Ninth Amendment rights, for example, simply because there are fewer repercussions for doing so. Perhaps also to a university, like its corporate counterpart, saving money is more important than protecting debatable liberties. This in some ways is not surprising.

But here is another curious paradox. Though this book has repeatedly condemned the policies that prohibit faculty-student romance, faculty and students themselves, with one obvious exception, have not risen to challenge them. The University of California at Berkeley, in particular, is well-known for voicing its dissent when cherished liberties are repressed; protests against the Vietnam War and the University of California loyalty oaths are cases in point. Why the silence now?

Perhaps the constituency (faculty and students in romantic relationships) is so small that a movement never materialized. All the ballyhoo notwithstanding, this is simply a small minority at best. It is also noteworthy that the subject matter is taboo, perchance making people reluctant to discuss it, which if true, is regrettable, since debate perishes accordingly. Finally, it is crucial to once again stress that there are considerable risks for challenging policies relating to sexual conduct, the least of which being the question of motives. As noted previously, there is the presumption of guilt by association. If you oppose sodomy laws or support same-sex marriage, you must be gay. The same presumably must be true if you challenge the faculty-student romance policy. A personal interest must be at stake. Consequently, many people avoid challenging sex-related laws and policies because they prefer to keep their private life private, or alternatively, because they do not want suspicions (such as being gay) directed at them. It is also worth mentioning that sexual "blue laws," for instance, that criminalize behaviors such as fornication and oral sex continue to persist, although they are rarely enforced, because politicians do not crusade to remove them either.

The paradox is that professors, often rewarded for being outspoken, thrive on controversy. The aforementioned romance policies, it would appear, would be ripe for the taking, particularly at the University of California, which is also one of the most liberal institutions in the United States. Surely other factors must have contributed to the absence of opposition besides discretion about one's private life?

War and Money

The answer, ostensibly, is twofold. First, the University of California romance policy was pushed into service during the initial stages of the war with Iraq and the occupational aftermath. It was a time when many civil liberties were sacrificed in the service of the "war on terror." By no stretch of the imagination, however, should faculty-student romance be one of them—unless, of course, the spillover effect of curtailing civil liberties during a time of war was so pernicious that it normalized the suppression of other unrelated rights. Romance is conceivably an absurd example of this.

It is also important to note that this policy was put in place when the University of California faced a $400 million budget cut, again suggesting that one of the primary motives for the romance policy, at least where the University of California is concerned, was financial. The motive itself is not problematic, since financial security is essential to a university's educational mission. It is simply the policy of prohibiting consensual romance that represents the problem. Though an expedient way to minimize civil liability, it sacrifices an essential liberty when alternative solutions would have sufficed.

All of that notwithstanding, the timing and ultimate success of the University of California policy per se can be best understood, I believe, in terms of the initial invasion of Iraq. The University of California's previous financial challenges during the early 1990s did not produce this policy, even though such policies existed elsewhere in the nation and sexual harassment lawsuits proliferated.

In a nutshell, here is the argument. University of California faculty and students lost their right to romantic relationships in order to further protect the university from civil litigation. Yet the success of this strategy depended on a unique cultural climate: the incipient war on terror and the invasion of Iraq. This climate permitted, regrettably in retrospect, the sacrifice of certain civil liberties. Romance was paradoxically one of them because it obstructed a "governmental" objective—that is, to reduce costs.

This is certainly not the first time that U.S. citizens have sacrificed their liberties (equally paradoxical) to make conscientious choices when war prevailed. Madison, concerned with the Alien and Sedition Acts (which were produced and justified by fears of a war with France), prophesied the following in a letter written to Jefferson on May 13, 1798: "Perhaps it is a universal truth that the loss of liberty at home is to be charged to provisions against danger, real or pretended, from abroad." In the same letter, he explained this principle as follows: "The management of foreign relations appears to be the most susceptible of abuse of all trusts committed to a Government, because they can be concealed or disclosed, or disclosed in such parts and at such times as will best suit particular views; and because the body of the people are less capable of judging, and are more under the influence of prejudices."[22]

The Alien and Sedition Acts

When cherished liberties crumble, including the romantic choice on a college campus, discussion always profits from a careful examination of the Alien and Seditions Acts of 1798. The controversy surrounding these acts helps to clarify the concept of liberty itself, aided in large part by Madison's and Jefferson's extensive written commentary in both public and private documents. These documents (notably the Kentucky and Virginia Resolutions) are particularly crucial because they provide insight into why our liberties were protected in the first place, and why these liberties represent the bedrock of U.S. jurisprudence.

Second, the Alien and Sedition Acts were ultimately applied in such an extreme, and arguably absurd, manner that they draw obvious parallel to this discussion about romance in the ivory tower. President John Adams in effect said, "Nobody can criticize me, particularly Republicans." This sentiment bears a striking resemblance to universities now saying, "No more consensual romance between professors and students." Both prohibit a fundamental conscientious choice and both capitalize on wartime hysteria (at least to the extent to which the latter went unchallenged).

It should be noted at the outset that prosecutions for seditious libel against government officials began prior to the passage of the Alien and Sedition Acts, and were based on the premise that there was a common law of the United States that gave authority to the federal courts to punish crimes other than those defined by federal statutes. Federal Circuit Court Judge Richard Peters, in *United States v. Worrall* (1798), summarized this position as follows:

The power to punish misdemeanors, is originally and strictly a common law power; of which, I think, the United States are constitutionally possessed. Congress in the form of a legislative act might have exercised it; but it may, also, in my opinion be enforced in a course of judicial proceeding. Whenever an offense aims at the subversion of any federal institution, or at the corruption of its public officers, it is an offense against the well-being of the United States; from its very nature, it is cognizable under their authority; and, consequently, it is within the jurisdiction of this Court, by virtue of the 11th section of the Judicial Act.[23]

Interestingly, this conclusion, drawing on common law, was not particularly effective in implementing seditious libel prosecutions. The Federalist Party, which dominated the government, therefore took the next step, and enacted the Alien and Sedition Acts. The purpose, they said, was to preserve the "well-being" of government. Curtailing speech, it was presumed, would accomplish this goal, much like curtailing romance preserves the well-being (at least financially) of university education, as asserted above. Both also had less noble agendas in mind.

There were, in fact, four separate acts that make up the Alien and Sedition Acts. The Naturalization Act (1 Stat. 566 [1798]), the Alien Act (1 Stat. 570 [1798]), the Alien Enemies Act (1 Stat. 577 [1798]), and the Sedition Act (1 Stat. 596 [1798]). Their purview was as follows. The Naturalization Act extended the time frame (from five to fourteen years) for the residence requirement necessary for citizenship. The Alien Act gave the president authority to deport any alien who was considered dangerous to the peace and safety of the United States. The Alien Enemies Act authorized the incarceration and banishment of aliens in the time of war. And finally, the Sedition Act (sedition meaning illegal acts designed to disrupt and overthrow the government) targeted what it called "domestic traitors." It made it a federal crime to dictate or publish "any false, scandalous, and malicious writing" against the government, Congress, or the president.[24]

The backdrop to these acts was the French declaration of war with Great Britain in 1793. Republicans, inspired by Jefferson and Madison, supported the French, whereas President Adams and his Federalist Party favored the British. When French-American relations deteriorated, the Federalists exploited anti-French sentiment to pass the Alien and Sedition Acts.

This was undoubtedly an auspicious moment. It was now a federal crime to criticize President Adams. Political commentary, both high and low, not surprisingly crumbled accordingly. For example, four of the five editors of the largest Republican newspapers were imprisoned.[25]

Although the Alien and Sedition Acts did not lead to insurrection, they did lead to the Kentucky and Virginia Resolutions. These resolutions—written largely by Jefferson and Madison, respectively—were designed to reassert constitutional liberties through the jurisdiction of states rights. While seditious libel was largely the incentive for these resolutions, it should be noted that the corruption of federal governmental power more generally was the overriding consideration. The resolutions themselves are therefore relevant to all liberties abated by governments—the loss of consensual romance in the ivory tower no less than the loss of speech. As such, they are now discussed in depth. As asserted repeatedly throughout this book, even though the subject matter appears trivial, the question of where the power to make choices resides is not. These resolutions and the conditions that precipitated them ultimately speak to this issue.

Judicial Review

Before turning to the resolutions themselves, it is important to understand the steps that were taken to corrupt federal power in the first place. This was most evident within the Federalist judiciary. For instance, to successfully implement convictions for sedition, the Federalist judiciary packed juries, controlled judicial appointments, and exercised the power of judicial review (well in advance of *Marbury v. Madison*). The latter is evident in the following example, drawn from Justice Samvel Chase, who apparently never met a Republican newspaper editor he didn't like.

James T. Callender was a Republican author of considerable notoriety, particularly for his highly critical comments about the Adams administration. His flair, not surprisingly, was unappreciated by the Federalists, earning Callender the charge of seditious libel.

In Callender's trial, his defense attorney argued that the jury, if it regarded the Sedition Act as being contrary to the Constitution (the First Amendment, in particular), could declare the law void and refuse to convict Callender under it.

Justice Chase was not persuaded. He asserted,

I cannot believe that any person...will maintain that a petit jury can rightfully exercise the power granted by the Constitution to the federal judiciary.... [Thus] I draw the conclusion, that the judicial power of the United States is the only proper and competent authority to decide whether any statute made by Congress (or any state legislatures) is contrary to, or in violation of, the federal Constitution.[26]

This conclusion, which is the essence of *judicial review*, was made by a politically avenging Federalist justice of considerable notoriety (who was, incidentally, eventually impeached), and gave enormous pause to the Republican Party, especially because it was invoked in the context of limiting political opposition.

The Supreme Court was not, I should add, by any stretch of the imagination a paragon of virtue under the Adams administration. Judicial review therefore created alarm because it represented a blatantly biased governmental body claiming absolute authority for interpreting the Constitution.

What, then, was the alternative?

At this stage of our constitutional history, there were at least three competitors vying for the prize of being the final arbiter of the Constitution. The Callender case introduced two of them: jury review and judicial review. The states' right to determine the constitutionality of federal legislation (which will now be called *states review*) was a third competitor as well. There is also some evidence that a fourth contestant (the president, or *presidential review*) wanted to assume this prize too. Though the Supreme Court obviously won the contest, hence the supremacy of judicial review, it did not, as is repeatedly told, invent this argument for the purpose of resolving *Marbury v. Madison*. Instead, Supreme Court justices had been "competing" with this contention well in advance of this infamous litigation, with the sedition trials (Callender, in particular) that upheld the constitutionality of an act of Congress in violation of the First Amendment being a case in point.

All of this, as one might imagine, was deeply and personally distressing to both Jefferson and Madison. When the alien bills were first introduced in Congress, Jefferson claimed in a letter to his daughter that he "never was more home-sick or heart-sick. The life of this place is particularly hateful to me."[27]

Jefferson's reaction to the Sedition Act was even worse. Though anti-French sentiment was high, it is important to emphasize that there was no war with France, or even a declaration of such. This was, paradoxically, the only instance in U.S. history when the legislature created a law for treason in peacetime.[28]

The distress for Jefferson was particularly noteworthy because even before Congress passed the Sedition Act, the Federalists had arrested the editor (Benjamin Franklin Bache) of the leading Jeffersonian newspaper for seditious libel.

What was Bache's crime? A misunderstanding, it seems, of the First Amendment. Bache knowingly criticized the president and the executive government.

Worse yet, Jefferson himself was accused as an accomplice to Bache. When the House of Representatives debated the Sedition Act, John Allen of Connecticut implied, at least discreetly, that Vice President Jefferson was intimately connected with Bache. Bache, Allen proclaimed, was the "[toxin] of insurrection," and Jefferson, though not named as such, was implicated as the person who walked the streets arm in arm and held closeted midnight vigils with him. The *Porcupine's Gazette*, in a similar fashion, chastised Jefferson as a confidant of Bache, claiming that both men were part of a treasonable conspiracy that represented a considerable threat to the United States.

On learning of these accusations from Republican congress person Willie Smith, Jefferson replied in return mail as follows: "If the receipt of visits in my public room, the door continuing free to every one who should call at the same time, may be called *closeting*, then it is true that I was *closeted* with every person who visited me; in no other sense is it true as to any person." He did, however, admit to seeing and admiring Bache, calling him an able and principled person "most friendly to liberty and our present form of government. Mr. Bache has another claim on my respect, as being the grandson of Dr. Franklin, the greatest man and ornament of the age and country in which he lived."[29]

On the other hand, in the same letter Jefferson was adamant in proclaiming that public office necessitates criticism, both public and private. This is obviously a First Amendment argument. Jefferson did not need the protection of sedition to silence his critics. In fact, he believed that it was his duty as a government official to submit to whatever the "public think proper to call to its councils."[30]

It is crucial to once again underscore a parallel to the loss of romance in the ivory tower. Universities now claim that they need the protection of such policies to accomplish their educational mission, much like the government needed the protection of sedition. Neither, it is now asserted, are so fragile that they would go asunder if free speech, or the freedom to romance, prevailed. Neither, it is also claimed, believed as much. Instead, the rhetoric in both cases is clearly designed to serve a more pedestrian objective: to silence critics or save money.

A final bit of insult occurred with the date of passage of the Sedition Act on July 4, 1798. This date undoubtedly grieved Jefferson, coming twenty-two years to the day of the Declaration of Independence. (Even more ironic is the fact that Jefferson's death occurred on July 4 as well, as did former President Adams several hours later, both on the fiftieth anniversary celebration of the Declaration of Independence.)

Rising to the Challenge: The Kentucky and Virginia Resolutions

Jefferson, with Madison's help, fought the Sedition Act with an alternative to judicial review. For convenience sake, as mentioned above, their argument is being labeled states review. As noted previously, judicial review presumes that the Supreme Court is the final arbiter of the Constitution. States review, in contrast, maintains that individual states can challenge the constitutionality of federal legislation if such legislation usurps the rights of individuals residing in a particular state, or if it usurps the powers of that state. Relying heavily on the Tenth Amendment, which proclaims that "the powers not delegated to the U.S. government, nor prohibited by it to the states, are reserved to the states respectively, or to the people," Jefferson and Madison attempted to overturn the Sedition Act as a violation of states rights.

Here is the argument in a nutshell. The First Amendment to the Constitution indicates that Congress should make no law abridging the freedom of speech. Hence, on reading this amendment, it is not unreasonable to conclude that Congress was never given the power to abridge speech, presumably including criticism of the president. If it is true that Congress does not have this power, the question then becomes, Where does this power reside? (A question, incidentally, that is at the heart of the present book as well.) The Tenth Amendment, one could allege, indicates that the power is reserved to the states or the people. Furthermore, since it is an individual right (secured by the First Amendment to participate in political debate), the relevance of governmental power is to *preserve* the right to speech. The Sedition Act is therefore a dual corruption of the Constitution because it tramples the right to free speech and presumes that the federal government has the power to do it.

Jefferson and Madison protested. Their strategy, as mentioned above, was the assertion of states rights. Though it may seem paradoxical that Madison, the architect of the Constitution, would revert to states rights, it is by no means inconsistent with his general philosophical position. According to Madison, the Constitution was designed to provide a strong but circumscribed federal government. The balance of powers was essential to this system. This included the elevation of individual rights as an additional means of *limiting* the power of the government. Since Madison feared that the greatest threat to the United States was the tyranny of the majority over the minority, the competing interests of the three branches of the federal government, coupled with the salience of the natural rights of U.S. citizens, the vested interests of each and every state, and so forth, would at least collectively put constraints on the ability to form or sustain a viable majority. Consequently, when Madison and Jefferson suspected that a majority from the federal government was exerting undue (and unconstitutional) power through the Sedition Act, they sought to give advantage to a neglected aspect of this equation: states rights. Thus, at the very least, states rights are an essential element of maintaining a balance of power that was critical to a properly functioning republic.

As mentioned previously, the specific vehicles for challenging the Sedition Act were known as the Kentucky and Virginia Resolutions. Jefferson wrote the former, and Madison the latter. In a preliminary draft of the Kentucky Resolution, Jefferson argued that a state legislature had the power to criticize a federal measure (thereby circumventing sedition itself) as well as the capability to judge its validity and enforceability (i.e., state review). Jefferson reasoned that since the federal government was in essence a "compact" among the state governments, each member of this compact had an equal right to judge infractions and levy consequences. This conclusion obviously predates the supremacy of judicial review, but it is worth reiterating that the conclusion itself is identical to the powers now attributed to the Supreme Court. Hence, Jefferson used state review to contend that since the federal government surpassed its delegated powers, the act was unconstitutional and the rightful remedy was its nullification.[31]

When the resolution itself was presented in Kentucky, however, the reference to nullification (and resistance to enforcement) was dropped in favor of urging senators and representatives to seek repeal of this legislation in Congress. Since Jefferson was not present, nor proclaimed as author of the resolutions, it was concluded, wisely no doubt, that it is prudent neither to defy federal law nor undermine the union of the states.

Interestingly, Madison agreed. The Virginia Resolutions, which did not name Madison as author as well, began with a declaration of support for the United States, but asserted that the Alien and Sedition Acts were "alarming infractions" of the Constitution. Hence, the resolutions called on the remaining states to join Virginia in declaring the acts unconstitutional, and restoring the rights and liberties reserved to the states and the people.

To emphasize this point, Madison wrote a detailed *Report on the Alien and Sedition Act* (January 7, 1800). It is unquestionably an extraordinary document. It offers a forum for Madison to set the record straight about the common law, prior restraint, the freedom of the press, the purpose of the Constitution, and the sanctity of the rights and powers retained by the people, all as a backdrop to his repudiation of the Alien and Sedition Acts. It is forceful, systematic, and erudite, and obviously relevant to the fundamental issues raised here. It is also written with considerable aplomb.

Besides being the architect of the Constitution, Madison was the primary note taker at the federal constitutional convention. This was certainly an advantage when it came to commenting on the Constitution and its proceedings. Madison ultimately was in a class by himself.

Taking exception to the Alien and Sedition Acts, Madison asserted that when the Constitution was under discussion there was concern that the freedom of press would be constrained by Congress, particularly under the guise of making laws it deemed necessary for carrying out enumerated powers. In response to this concern, Madison noted that

it was invariably urged to be a fundamental characteristic principle of the constitution; that all powers not given by it, were reserved; that no powers were given beyond those enumerated in the constitution, and such as were fairly incident to them; that the power over the rights in question, and particularly over the press, was neither among the enumerated powers, nor incident to any of them; and consequently that an exercise of any such power, would be a manifest usurpation. It is painful to remark, how much the arguments now employed in behalf of the sedition act, are at variance with the reasoning which then justified the constitution, and invited its ratification.[32]

Of particular significance is the phrase "a fundamental characteristic principle of the constitution." This implies, at least according to Madison, that protecting the *unremunerated* rights and powers of the people was no less basic to the Constitution than the formation of the government itself. This conclusion is also manifest in the Ninth and Tenth Amendments, which explicitly emphasize Madison's point. What makes this especially curious and disheartening, however, is that the judiciary (even to this day) has effectively nullified these amendments. People's rights, sexual and romantic rights among them, are usually held hostage by a government unwilling to acknowledge anything but enumerated rights. This now appears in direct opposition to the intent specified by Madison as well as the Ninth and Tenth Amendments themselves.

Where the freedom of the press in particular is concerned, Madison was no less emphatic. He is quoted here at length to demonstrate the force of his opinion.

The first Congress that assembled under the constitution, proposed certain amendments which have since, by necessary ratifications, been made a part of it; among which amendments is the article containing, among other prohibitions on Congress, an express declaration that they should make no law abridging the freedom of press.

Without tracing farther the evidence on this subject, it would seem scarcely possible to doubt, that no power whatever over the press, was supposed to be delegated by the constitution, as it originally stood; and that the amendment was intended as a positive and absolute reservation of it.

But the evidence is still stronger. The proposition of amendments made by Congress, is introduced in the following terms: "The Conventions of a number of states having at the time of their adopting the Constitution, expressed a desire, in order to prevent misconstructions or abuse of its powers, that further declaratory and restrictive clauses should be added; and as extending the ground of public confidence in the government, will best ensure the beneficent ends of its institutions."

Here is the most satisfactory and authentic proof, that the several amendments proposed, were to be considered as either declaratory or restrictive; and whether the one or the other, as corresponding with the desire expressed by a number of the states, and as extending the ground of public confidence in the government.[33]

Continuing this theme more generally, Madison again asserts, "The constitution alone can answer this question. If no such power be expressly delegated, and it be not both necessary and proper to carry into execution an express power; above all, if it be expressly forbidden by a declaratory amendment to the constitution, the answer must be, that the federal government is destitute of all such authority."[34]

The take-home message being that if it is not in the Constitution, it belongs to the people. Furthermore, if the Constitution forbids it, it is meant to be forbidden.

The freedom of the press is particularly significant because Madison believed it to be one of the "great remedial rights of the people." It is, he stressed, "indispensable to the just exercise of their electoral rights." Coverage of political candidates, newcomers and incumbents alike, is the grist of the voting mill, so to speak. If the freedom of the press were abridged, Madison concludes, it would "destroy our free system of government." The Sedition Act especially would destroy the government because Madison felt it would give unfair advantage to incumbents who would be "protected" from criticism by sedition, competing against candidates running for office who are not protected by such.

Against the claim that the press has and will continue to act irresponsibly, Madison introduced his version of a "marketplace of ideas," organized instead around the question of whether "to prune or not to prune." We permit the freedom of the press (and by extension, speech) despite its abuses because, as Madison observed,

some degree of abuse is inseparable from the proper use of every thing; and in no instance is this more true, than in that of the press. It has accordingly been decided by the practice of the states, that it is better to leave a few of its noxious branches, to their luxuriant growth, than by pruning them away, to injure the vigor of those yielding the proper fruits. And can the wisdom of this policy be doubted by any who reflect, that to the press alone, chequered as it is with abuses, the world is indebted for all the triumphs which have been gained by reason and humanity, over error and oppression; who reflect that to the same beneficent source, the United States owe much of the lights which conducted them to the rank of a free and independent nation; and which have improved their political system, into a shape so auspicious to their happiness.[35]

The pruning metaphor is no less relevant to speech than it is to consensual romance in the ivory tower. Noxious branches exist within both, the power differential between a professor and a student being a prime example of the latter. Accordingly, universities have now pruned so excessively that they eliminated the liberty to make conscientious choices about romance—which is no less absurd than the prohibition against criticizing the president. Moreover, we are arguably equally indebted to the triumphs of romance as we are to speech. The Sedition Act clearly damaged the very foundation of the marketplace of ideas, and similarly, I believe that university consensual romance prohibitions now destroy the very process by which we define the self, the act of making conscientious choices.

Returning to Madison's argument, there is clearly no constitutional basis for the Sedition Act. Quite to the contrary, the Constitution explicitly forbids it. How, then, was the Sedition Act defended?

Interestingly, those who promoted the Sedition Act defended it by reference to the common law. Originating in England, the common law is of judicial origin and is based on judicial precedent. It is distinct from statutory law, which is enacted through legislation. Common law, in essence, is what a judge decides in the courtroom, and presumably is based on a system of flexible principles derived from justice, reason, and common sense. This very process is what defenders of the Sedition Act claimed for its legitimacy.

Madison repudiated this as a defense, contending that the United States, as a brand-new entity, did not in fact have a common law. For example, he reminded his readers that "the common law was not the same in any two of the colonies; in some, the modifications were materially and extensively different. There was no common legislature, by which a common will, could be expressed in the form of law; nor any common magistery, by which such a law could be carried into practice. The will of each colony alone and separately, had its organs for these purposes."[36] Hence, in the absence of a shared common law tradition, it was specious to claim that there was a common law in the first place, let alone a common law that would serve as a foundation for the Sedition Act.

Madison's conclusion about the common law was especially significant for the issue of prior restraint. Defenders of the

Sedition Act argued that the phrase "Congress could make no law ... abridging" was derivative of a common law perspective against prior restraint. Thus, according to this assertion, the sole intent of this phrase was to limit Congress from making prior restraint laws. Congress could, however, make laws punishing violations when speech occurred or the press published, for example, as long as prior restraints did not exist.

Madison concluded that this interpretation was equally ludicrous. He commented,

The freedom of the press under the common law, is, in the defenses of the sedition act, made to consist in an exemption from all *previous* restraint on printed publications, by persons authorized to inspect and prohibit them. It appears to the committee, that this idea of the freedom of the press can never be admitted to be the American idea of it; since a law inflicting penalties on printed publications, would have a similar effect with a law authorizing a previous restraint on them. It would be a mockery to say, that no law should be passed, preventing publications from being made, but that laws might be passed for punishing them in case they should be made.[37]

It is also interesting to note that Madison's concern with prior restraint led to the following statement on the basic principle of our rights and freedoms: "In the United States ... the people, not the government, possess the absolute sovereignty. The legislature, no less than the executive, is under limitations of power. Encroachments are regarded as possible from the one, as well as from the other. Hence in the United States, the great and essential rights of the people are secured against the legislature, as well as executive ambition. They are secured, not by laws paramount to prerogative; but by constitution paramount to laws."[38] As mentioned above, at least according to Madison, the fundamental principle of the Constitution is to limit the powers of the government, and protect "the great and essential rights of the people."

Consensual romance, I now assert, is invariably one of those rights.

Finally, it is also worth noting that Madison considered the freedom of the press and the freedom of conscience to be closely related. Though the focal point of the Virginia Resolutions was obviously the press (and the Alien and Sedition Acts more specifically), the concept of conscience is conspicuously present as well, suggesting that Madison was giving similar footing to both. Here is what he wrote: "That this state having by its Convention, which ratified the Federal Constitution expressly declared, that among other essential rights, 'the liberty of conscience and of the press cannot be canceled, abridged, restrained or modified by any authority of the United States.'"[39] In my view, this should include the governing bodies of a university, which undoubtedly hold the freedom of the press sacred, but apparently fail to appreciate the significance of the liberty of conscience as well.

The association between conscience and the press is also illustrated in Virginia's statement ratifying the federal Constitution itself. It asserted: "That therefore, no right of any denomination can be canceled, abridged, restrained or modified, by the Congress, by the Senate or House of Representatives acting in any capacity, by the president, or any department or officer in the United States, except in those instances in which power is given by the constitution for those purposes; and, that among other essential rights, the liberty of conscience and of press, cannot be canceled, abridged, restrained or modified by any authority of the United States."[40] It is especially important to point out that this statement does not conflate religion ("no right of any denomination") with the liberty of conscience, instead treating the latter as an adjunct to the freedom of the press.

Lastly, Madison's own language is perhaps the most forceful of all on the relationship between the freedoms of the press and conscience:

Words could not well express, in fuller or more forcible manner, the understanding of the convention, that the liberty of conscience and the freedom of press, were *equally* and *completely* exempted from all authority whatever of the United States...both of these rights, liberty of conscience and of the press, rest equally on the original ground of not being delegated by the constitution, and consequently withheld from the government. Any construction therefore, that would attack this original security for the one must have the like effect on the other.[41]

Clearly, the liberty of conscience, like the freedom of the press, certainly according to Madison, is exempt from governmental intrusion. If one concedes that the liberty of conscience extends beyond the scope of religion, the choices made about consensual sex and romance are an obvious component of such.

This conclusion, of course, begs the question of whether conscience was merely a synonym for religion. Perhaps Madison was simply emphasizing that the Constitution was designed to protect the freedom of the press and the freedom of religion equally. The First Amendment suggests as much, as do the instances where the words conscience and religion are used interchangeably.

As indicated above, however, at least according to Madison, religion and conscience were clearly distinct entities. The First Amendment evidently went through many permutations before being ratified. It is therefore perhaps more useful to examine an early draft of the Bill of Rights, written expressly by Madison, to gain insight into his own perspective.

Proposed to the House of Representatives on June 8, 1789, the Bill of Rights stated: "Fourthly. That in article 1st, section 9, between clauses 3 and 4 [of the Constitution], be inserted these clauses, to wit, The civil rights of none shall be abridged on account of religious belief or worship, nor shall any national religion be established, nor shall the full and equal rights of conscience be in any manner, or on any pretext infringed."[42] In this context, Madison conceptualized three separate rights: no discrimination based on religious choice; no national religion (which could exert pressure on religious choice); and no infringement of the full and equal rights of conscience (that is, the right to make choices based on one's personal conscience, as opposed to pressure from or requirements by governments, religions, etc.). Hence, for Madison, religion and conscience were distinct entities—this being necessary in order to ensure that the one (religion) did not unduly influence the other (making choices based on one's personal conscience).

This is not surprising. Religions, national and otherwise, could be just as oppressive as governments. Thus, to ensure "life, liberty, and the pursuit of happiness," the United States clearly and purposely separated church and state.

In summation, the Alien and Sedition Acts represent the epitome of an unconstitutional abridgment of the freedoms of speech and the press. The Kentucky and Virginia Resolutions, in turn, reassert state and individual rights. This chapter in U.S. history confirms once again that power, like love, is blind.

The Resolution

Though the Alien and Sedition Acts were repealed in the following administration, seditious libel itself was not banished by the Supreme Court until 1964, in *New York Times Co. v. Sullivan*. This case is key in the history of U.S. jurisprudence because it involved an advertisement criticizing the arrest of Martin Luther King Jr.[43] It is now being examined because it represents an apt metaphor for the issue of consensual romance in the ivory tower by demonstrating that liberty needs "breathing space" in order to survive.

In 1960, King was arrested in Alabama and charged with perjury. A committee, formed in New York City, and made up of civil rights workers and various celebrities, was formed to generate financial assistance for his defense. To gain recognition, they took out a full-page *New York Times* advertisement titled "Heed Their Rising Voices" that described King's arrest and other related events.

A problem arose, however, with the question of whether the advertisement depicted the "related events" accurately. For instance, the advertisement claimed that: Alabama students protesting segregation sang "My Country, 'Tis of Thee" on the steps of the Alabama State House; students were expelled from campus for leading the protest; the entire student body of Alabama State College protested the expulsions; armed police ringed the campus, padlocked the dining hall to starve students into submission, bombed King's house, and assaulted King as well; and the police arrested King seven times for speeding, loitering, and other dubious behaviors.

L. B. Sullivan, an elected commissioner of Montgomery, Alabama, was outraged. The description of these related events, he asserted, was false. As a supervisor of the Montgomery police department, he also felt that this advertisement, insinuating police abuse, defamed him personally. Consequently, he filed a libel action against the *New York Times* in Alabama State Court.

It should be noted that Sullivan was not mentioned, certainly by name, in the advertisement. This is normally a significant omission in libel litigation. Yet a jury could conclude that the omission of his name was immaterial if it believed that readers would still identify Sullivan as instrumental in police actions. Furthermore, if the jury reached this conclusion, Sullivan could then claim that his professional reputation had been sullied (i.e., the ad was libelous per se).

Truth, on the other hand, is an effective defense against this claim. If indeed the advertisement spoke the truth, and nothing but the truth, it would be difficult to prove libel, even if Sullivan was named therein.

Unfortunately, in this particular case there were so many factual errors in the ad that "truth" was not a viable defense for the *New York Times*. For example, the students sang "The Star-Spangled Banner," not "My Country, 'Tis of Thee." Similarly, students were expelled for requesting service at a segregated lunch counter, not for leading a protest at the capitol; the entire body of Alabama State College did not protest the expulsions (although a "majority" did); the police did not ring the campus but were instead deployed nearby; and King was arrested four times, not seven.

These discrepancies are superficial, and while several states recognize such errors as trivial, or more precisely "good faith" in the process of criticizing public officials, Alabama was not one of them. Hence, Sullivan succeeded; an Alabama jury awarded him $500,000.

This case was appealed and eventually made its way in 1964 to the Supreme Court. Interestingly, the Supreme Court equated the Alabama decision with the Sedition Act of 1798. In making this comparison, the Court emphasized that the Sedition Act had already been invalidated "in the court of history" because it precluded "criticism of government and public officials."[44]

The *New York Times* thereby prevailed. The Supreme Court ruled that the Alabama law violated the First Amendment. In doing so, however, the Court had to first distance itself from several previous rulings that held that libelous remarks are not constitutionally protected speech (e.g., *Beauharnais v. Illinois* [1952]). Rejecting those prior decisions, the Court now declared that like the "various other formulae for the repression of expression that have been challenged in this Court, libel can claim no talismanic immunity from constitutional limitations." Instead, libel "must be measured by standards that satisfy the First Amendment."[45]

This case also removed trivial errors as a basis for libel. Justice William Brennan noted that "erroneous statement is inevitable in free debate," and as such, even error needs to be "protected if the freedoms of expression are to have 'breathing space' that they need . . . to survive."[46]

Finally, Brennan summarized the Court's decision as follows: "We consider this case against the background of a profound national commitment to the principle that debate on public issues should be uninhibited, robust, and wide-open, and that it may well include vehement, caustic, and sometimes unpleasantly sharp attacks on government and public officials."[47]

Return to Romance

What, then, can we conclude thus far? Where the First Amendment is concerned, it seems that the good outweighs the bad. To this I would add the following: according to the great rights invoked by Madison, it is no less true of the Ninth Amendment than the First. Meaning that consensual sex and romance are no less hallowed than speech, the press, and religion. Here is the analogy.

Romance between professors and students can go awry. It is the nature of such things. A status difference, as noted previously, exists as well. There are the added problems of favoritism and supervision. All of this notwithstanding, however, it is infinitely better to accept the "unpleasant"—in this case, the existence of romance in the ivory tower (and thereby give it breathing space)—than to prohibit a fundamental right to think, choose, and judge whom to love. Personal autonomy ultimately depends on it.

Moreover, to constrain lunch seating is no less an abridgment of liberty than it is to restrict whom to romance. Both represent governing bodies making preemptive constraints on choice. Though alternatives exist for both, they are decidedly less convenient and desirable. Liberty therefore fails accordingly. This is true for free speech—and consensual romance as well.

How, then, should we protect the privilege of choice? Or alternatively, how do we protect the expression of individual rights? The answer in both cases as I have repeatedly asserted, is to protect the rights and liberty of conscience.

Jefferson, it should be noted, concluded similarly: "We are bound, you, I, and every one, to make common cause, even with error itself, to maintain the common right of freedom of conscience."[48]

The next chapter is devoted to this subject.

2

Liberty of Conscience

There are three essential components to the theory presented thus far. First, that the rights of conscience are a constituent part of the bedrock of our constitutional heritage (the First and Ninth Amendments in particular). Second, the rights of conscience are distinct from and ultimately supersede the freedoms associated with religion. Lastly, the rights of conscience can be extended to all matters of substance that require serious deliberations about right and wrong, consensual sex and romance included.

To answer the question posed at the beginning of this book—Where does the power to make the choice about romance reside?—I again assert that it is with the individual—in particular, the rights of conscience. The conscience protects the right to make romantic choices without interference or refutation by governmental and institutional entities.

In this chapter I will now consider the various origins of the term conscience, and thereafter examine how it became integrated into the U.S. political zeitgeist. This is important because the argument introduced herein relies in large part on the rights of conscience. This is not to say that the argument is solely dependent on crafting a defendable legal rationale for such rights; quite to the contrary. Instead, it is the logic of the argument that is hopefully persuasive. The legal scholarship necessary to sustain it will have to await authors with greater expertise. Suffice it to say that the present book simply introduces relevant legal issues in the service of making its points about the rights of conscience.

I am also extending that strategy in the present chapter by examining the broader literatures on the rights of conscience. Considerable attention therefore will be devoted to Roger Williams, whose ideas were to some extent the springboard for such. Other texts and writers will be introduced as well. Similarly, the term liberty will be closely scrutinized since it, too, is an essential part of the concept under consideration—that is, the liberty of conscience. Early American and more contemporary theorists (John Stuart Mill, Isaiah Berlin, and John Rawls) who have written about liberty and conscience also will be explored.

The Backstory

Though Madison and Jefferson campaigned repeatedly for the liberty of conscience, neither was the first American to publicly champion this cause. That honor instead goes to Williams, the founder of Rhode Island. He predated Madison and Jefferson by nearly one hundred and fifty years.

Before examining Williams, however, it might be useful to consider the meaning of the word conscience itself. The Greek word *syneidesis* and its Latin equivalent *conscientia* represent the foundations of the English word conscience. Neither, curiously, is an exact equivalent of such, but instead have various meanings, which bear some relationship to contemporary usage. For example, knowledge, self-knowledge, and consciousness are among the various translations of both *syneidesis* and *conscientia.* These definitions were eventually combined into the noun we use today.[1]

Merriam-Webster's Dictionary defines conscience as the faculty, power, or principle of a person that decides on the lawfulness or unlawfulness of one's actions, with a compulsion to do right. It also defines conscience as a moral judgment that prohibits or opposes the violation of a previously recognized ethical principle. What these definitions share in common, as indicated previously, is the process whereby a person uses their knowledge and feelings to judge right from wrong, with the objective to pursue what one believes is right.

Conscience is clearly relevant to morality and religion too. Yet interestingly, the word conscience itself, or its equivalent, is virtually absent in the Old Testament. The judgment of actions is instead described in reference to the government or the law. Exceptions include the concept of heart, as in "David's heart smote him," meaning presumably that his heart acted as his conscience and made him feel bad.

The New Testament rarely mentions the word conscience either. When it appears, however, it does bear a resemblance to contemporary usage in the form of a moral judgment about the quality (right or wrong) of a conscious act. That exception notwithstanding, it is still the case that conscience is conspicuously missing in the Bible.[2]

Clearly, then, the widespread contemporary use of the concept of conscience and the legal implications of the liberty of conscience are not biblical in origin but rather are the consequence of two separate philosophical developments, both of which relate to the autonomy and independence of thought. Despite religious affiliations, humans over the centuries were increasingly deemed capable of self-regulation. A conscience therefore became a necessity, and was cultivated as such, through teaching and other forms of imitative learning as well as punishments, both civil and religious. Similarly, as citizens took more responsibility in their governance, a conscience was needed as well—to vote according to one's conscience being a case in point. As these customs grew, including choosing one's religion, and by implication one's God or the choice to forego both, the need to protect the choices made out of a careful deliberation of one's conscience became paramount.

The liberty of conscience is therefore, as repeatedly asserted, an explicit recognition of the capacity to distinguish right from wrong. More important, it also acknowledges that each person has the privilege, hence the liberty, to use that capacity without governmental or institutional interference. One of the main points of the present book is simply that the choices we make about God, no less than sex and romance, are the obvious beneficiaries of this principle.

Returning to Williams, it is essential to note that although Jefferson and Madison were highly rewarded for their philosophical contributions to the United States, both ascending to the presidency, Williams was less fortunate. He received, in October 1635, lifetime banishment from the Massachusetts Bay Colony.

In all fairness, Williams was not banished from the Massachusetts Bay Colony solely for his beliefs about the liberty of conscience. The colony lost patience with him for many reasons, particularly his constant challenges to religion and government, so much so, in fact, that they considered killing him. Williams fortunately escaped that fate.

Eventually, he landed on his feet, and shortly thereafter founded Providence, Rhode Island. Despite his lifetime banishment, Williams managed to be embraced once again by the Massachusetts Bay Colony (especially its governor) and the governing party more generally when his expertise in Indian affairs was critically needed.

To better understand Williams, it is perhaps useful to examine the first book he published, titled *A Key into the Language of America*. It is, ostensibly, a Native American dictionary—Algonquian words in particular. The reputation of the book, however, rests on Williams's anecdotal observations. England was especially intrigued by the image of a Cambridge-educated Christian living among Native Americans.

This book was not a mere travelogue, though. Williams had a deep and passionate interest in Native Americans, particularly their belief systems. In fact, he respected them so much that he saw it necessary to purchase his land from Native Americans prior to obtaining a British charter to govern it. The charter for Providence, Rhode Island, was therefore designed to protect his right to the land from other colonists.[3] Williams felt that any land, the Massachusetts Bay Colony included, that was not purchased directly from Native Americans was contraband.

Imagine, now, a deeply religious man, who was educated at Cambridge University, living among Native Americans because he was fascinated by their culture, forcefully arguing that America belonged to the indigenous peoples, and therefore the right to reside there must be obtained and purchased from them. This is a radical perspective for the twenty-first century; imagine its reception in the 1600s when British colonization was perceived to be a divine right.

Besides protecting their land, Williams also appreciated the culture and spiritual life of Native Americans. Take, for example, what is best described as Native American "meals on the run":

Parched meal, which is ready wholesome food, which they eat with little water, hot or cold. I have traveled with nearly 200 of them at once, near 100 miles through the woods, every man carrying a little basket of this at his back, and sometimes in a hollow leather girdle about his middle sufficient for a man three or four days.

With this provision, and their bow and arrows, are they ready for war and travel at an hour's warning. With a spoonful of water from the brook, have I made many a good dinner and supper.[4]

Similarly, note Williams's appreciation for the manner in which Native Americans treated him, or other guests: "It is a strange truth that a man shall generally find more free entertainment and refreshing [sic] amongst these barbarians than amongst thousands that call themselves Christians.[5]

Finally, Native American spiritual beliefs impressed him as well, due in large part to what he perceived as shared assumptions. This was particularly significant to Williams because he maintained, vehemently at times, that truth, and certainly spiritual truth, can be discovered without excessive scriptural intrusions, which clearly elevates the *role* of conscience. He was convinced in large part that the human spirit thrives, perhaps best, when left unfettered.[6]

It would not be surprising to discover that many readers have now concluded that Williams was an interesting and progressive young man. Though it is true, Williams was also an excruciatingly difficult person, and a religious fanatic to boot.

When Williams first arrived in the Massachusetts Bay Colony in 1631, he was applauded for his eloquence and education. When an opening for a pastor became available at the new church in Boston, Williams was offered the position, but turned it down.

Why? Williams declared, "I durst not officiate to an unseparated people, as, upon examination and conference, I found them to be."[7]

What, exactly, did Williams mean by "unseparated people"?

It turns out that he was a Separatist, which in essence meant that he believed that the Church of England was not a Christian church. If members of the Boston congregation held allegiance to the Church of England, it would make them, at least according to Williams, non-Christians. Williams declined their offer because he preferred to preach only to "true" Christians.

Protestants, at least during this era, believed that the Church of Rome (hence the Catholic Church) was the church of the Antichrist. When English monarchs (e.g., Mary Tudor) temporarily equated the Church of England with the (Antichrist) Church of Rome, the Church of England was forever tainted, at least according to the Separatists. Anyone who thereafter still adhered to the Church of England was a de facto agent of the Antichrist. Separatists had other complaints as well (including the "national" character of the Church of England, its methods of discipline, and so forth), all of which were fodder for their contempt.

Perhaps even more extreme was Williams's contention that only after a person repents the sin of worshipping in an Antichrist church (plus all of his other sins), can that person be admitted to a "true Christian" church membership. Or to put it in Williams's words, no former "whore" could be admitted to church membership "without sound Repentance for the filthiness of her skirts (Lament 1.) not only in actual whoredomes, but also in Whorish speeches, Gestures, Appearances, Provocation. And why should there be a greater strictness for the skirts of common whoredom, then of spiritual and soul Whoredome, against the chastity of God's worship."[8]

Comments such as these obviously have more appeal to Sigmund Freud than to civil libertarians. Williams, in fact, had a peculiar penchant for the liberal use of sexual imagery in the service of extreme religious fundamentalism.

Despite this fanaticism and other curiosities, Williams was also the first American, as noted previously, to champion the cause of the liberty of conscience. As paradoxical as it may now seem, the man who condemned Catholics and the Church of England as filthy "whores," and the man who was not particularly fond of Quakers either, did nonetheless champion the right to practice religion according to one's own conscience. He believed that "Papists, Protestants, Jews or Turks [should not] be forced to come to . . . Prayers or Worship; nor secondly, compelled from their own particular Prayers or Worship, if they practice any."[9]

This is clearly at the heart of contemporary notions of the freedom of religion, and more broadly, the rights and liberty of conscience. Namely, that you cannot be forced to practice a religion, nor conversely, be forced to alter your religious practice.

Williams also believed in the separation between church and state. People create governments, Williams asserted, but they cannot thereafter baptize them into Christian entities. Williams also explained that God's relationship to the people is solely through redemption, whereas governments are limited to implementing peace, justice, and civil order.[10] This distinction rests on a *spiritual* conclusion, whereby governments are excluded from religion, being irrelevant to either God or redemption. It is in sharp contrast to existing efforts to blend church and state through religious influence in secular politics.

Why was Williams so adamant about the liberty of conscience, despite his own severe religious prejudices?

The answer, I believe, is that Williams was so different, and extreme, in his own religious point of view that he wanted to protect his right to believe and preach as he wished. Since he also believed that most other men (and women too) did not deserve to be called Christians, and that most religions failed to uphold the Bible, Williams was perhaps protecting the liberty of conscience for the purely narcissistic reason that he viewed himself as a spokesperson for religious truth. That is, if Williams is protected by the liberty of conscience, so too, at least according to Williams's logic, is the word of God.[11]

Williams was obviously a fanatic about religion. Yet his passion for what he believed in, and his commitment not to be denied, fostered America's first advocate for religious freedom, particularly along the lines of protecting religious difference and exercising the right to use one's conscience as the arbiter for religious choice.

That notwithstanding, it is equally important to emphasize this perspective was also flourishing at approximately the same time in Europe as well. John Locke is a prime example, as evidenced in a May 16, 1699, letter to Samuel Bold. Locke states:

The first requisite to the profiting by books is not to judge of opinion by the authority of the writers. None have the right of dictating but God himself, and that because he is truth itself. All others have a right to be followed as far as I have, and no farther, i.e., as far as the evidence of what they say convinces, and of that my own understanding alone must be judge for me, and nothing else. If we made our own eyes our guides, admitted or rejected opinions only by the evidence of reason, we should neither embrace nor refuse any tenet, because we find it published by another, *what name or character so ever be was.*[12]

This sentiment clearly recognizes the value of individual judgment over and above the value of an authoritative text. Save for the word of God itself, all other proscriptions must be evaluated on their merit. It is ultimately the burden and the right of the individual to decide accordingly. Hence, though not explicitly mentioned as such, Locke certainly implies that one's conscience must serve as one's guide.

This belief, incidentally, gained prominence in seventeenth-century Europe, and England in particular, out of a recognition for a rational moral will. Morality, it was now believed, required independent thinking, as cited above. Books or structured guidelines were no longer sufficient to create a truly moral person who was incapable of thinking on their own. Developing a rational will, and the necessary independence of thought, was therefore a prerequisite for attaining moral and spiritual enlightenment.

The vagaries of life necessitated as much. Though many moral dilemmas can be anticipated and thereby proscribed, uncertainties exist as well. Individuals capable of making rational moral choices throughout the entire fabric of their life, it was now believed, attain a higher moral and spiritual development than those who cannot. Life in essence is a test of an individual's character, as evidenced through the acts of one's conscience.

By the end of the seventeenth century, the primacy of a self-governing moral will—a conscience, so to speak—as opposed to the supremacy of an authoritative text had become well embedded in English middle-class life. The following sermon by John Sharp (and paraphrased by Edmund Leites) is a case in point.

"The laws of our great Master are not like the laws of kingdoms, which are . . . wonderful nice, and critical, and particular in setting bounds to the practices of men." Loving one's neighbor is a duty, but we have no law of God that defines "how far we may seek our own, when our right cannot be obtained with prejudice to another, Prayer is required, but we have not any law of God which defines how often we are to pray." God commands temperance in both feelings and action, but does not define "to what degree we may be angry; or how we are to govern ourselves as to the quantity or kinds of our meat and drink;...or how splendid we may be in our apparel and equipage." All questions about limits, however, were unnecessary, Sharp said, if one's aim was to be thoroughly good. Uneducated as one may be "in the dry rules" of an authoritative text, "there is scarce any case to be put concerning an action, but it is very obvious without an instructor, to find out which side of the case, if it be chosen, will most minister to the ends of virtue, and religion, and charity. Or, if it not be obvious, then it is very certain the man needs not much deliberate about it, but may choose either side indifferently."[13]

This clearly says it all. Using our good conscience as a guide, we should have no difficulty making choices that promote "virtue, and religion, and charity." On the other hand, try as we might, if the moral choice is not apparent, than either choice should suffice.

Though it is obvious that a significant transition has now occurred from revering religious texts to promoting individual conscience, which certainly is fundamental to its eventual U.S. constitutional usage, the psychological manifestation of such also warrants comment. Williams and Locke, among others, are extolling the importance of psychological autonomy, not only for the sake of the personal satisfaction it might bring, but in terms of satisfying the quest for intellectual and spiritual truth. Both therefore emphasized the need for independence from authoritative, and thereby authoritarian, forms of thinking.

Reliance on one's own conscience also creates a boundary between the self and others. It creates a boundary between the self and "other" people as well as between our own opinion and that of "others" (particularly in speech or written text). Though we are obviously influenced by both sources, the recognition of the need and right (as made explicit within the U.S. constitutional archives) to make our own decisions is clearly a fundamental aspect of the liberty of conscience, and freedom more generally. This is no less so for the choices we construct about sex and romance, than for those we make about religion.

All of this notwithstanding, it is crucial to also reiterate that the liberty of conscience, certainly in the seventeenth century, was emphasized almost exclusively as either a higher form of moral development or a strategy for combating religious persecution.

Thinking on one's own, as cited above, is the more expansive and thereby superior form of moral deliberation when compared to the rigid recitation of a religious text. General notions of liberty and freedom, as applied to other aspects of life (e.g., speech, the press, etc.) are conspicuously missing at this point in time. Instead, relying on one's conscience, it was believed, is simply a better way of expressing God's will.

Similarly, in the seventeenth century the liberty of conscience was also presumed to be the best way of challenging religious persecution. This strategy is especially evident in the words of Leonard Busher, who in 1614 wrote the tract "Religion's Peace: A Plea for Liberty of Conscience." Busher states:

First—Because Christ hath not commanded any king, bishop, or minister to persecute the people for difference of judgment in matters of religion.

Secondly—Because Christ hath commanded his bishops and ministers to persuade prince and people to hear and believe the gospel, by his word and Spirit, and, as ambassadors for him, to beseech both prince and people to be reconciled unto God; and not, as tyrants, to force and constrain them by persecution.[14]

But even with these limited forms of interpretation, seeking spiritual development or challenging religious persecution, the liberty of conscience nevertheless represents a substantial break from earlier traditions and unquestionably ranks as an exercise of personal autonomy of the first order. Freedom to think on one's own, particularly about such weighty matters as God's redemption or perfection, is a giant step in favor of the psychologically autonomous person. And in that respect it mirrors two other major psychological transitions occurring almost contemporaneously in the development of autonomy: voting and science.

Fifty years before Locke wrote his letter to Bold, Thomas Rainborough, a member of the British Levellers party, noted in reference to voting that "every man born in England cannot, ought not, neither by the Law of God nor the Law of Nature, to be exempted from the choice of those who are to make laws for him to live under, and for him, for aught I know, to lose his life under."[15] The justification for this conclusion, once again, was the capacity for independent thinking.

Continuing, Rainborough asserted that "I *do* think the main cause why Almighty God gave men reason, it was that they should make use of that reason, and that they should improve it for that end and purpose that God gave it them."[16] Thus, our ability to think, make critical evaluations, and rely on our conscience in the choices we make (sentiments clearly advocated by Madison as well) are collectively the characteristics that entitle us to vote. And since we have those characteristics, we are entitled to participate in the choice of governmental representatives who will make the laws that determine how we live and die.

Voting, accordingly, is a quintessential act of independence. It is also a fundamental expression of autonomy, both from autocratic rule, which prohibits voting, and from all other citizens, by virtue of being an independent act. The liberty of conscience and voting are similar to the extent that they ac-knowledge the capacity for independent judgment, and the freedom from dependence on autocratic rule.

Finally, the scientific revolution shares common ground here as well. Like voting and the liberty of conscience, the birth of science was ultimately a supreme act of autonomy. Instead of a rigid adherence to ancient texts, Aristotelian deductive logic in particular, modern science was born when the inductive pro-cesses of observation and experimentation took precedence over the power of prior authority. What makes this particu-larly curious, but perhaps not surprising, is that Francis Bacon's scientific revolution also occurred in the seventeenth century; almost at the same time the liberty of conscience was being widely endorsed. Both are clearly changes in the service of autonomy. And when combined with suffrage, they create a profound change in independent thought. Choices about morality, governance, and scientific fact were now free of ex-cessive (or certainly exclusive) reliance on ancient (or omni-present) authority. Dependence on the past was reaching a saturation point. Independence and perhaps freedom more generally were now blossoming, or at the very least, were in their incipient stage of development in the premodern era.

These matters are obviously relevant to the thesis presented herein. First, they support and provide the historical back-ground to one of the basic components of the proposed argu-ment: that the liberty of conscience is not synonymous with religious freedom but instead is fundamental to the process by which personal autonomy is created as a result of the personal (as opposed to authoritative) deliberations of distinguishing right from wrong.

Second, this discussion suggests that the rights (and liberty) of conscience are relevant to other issues besides religion, thereby also laying the groundwork for the present suggestion that it should be extended to consensual romance and sex as well. Both depend on the independence of thought and feeling, and deserve careful deliberation too. Both also precipitate relevant actions, either romantic behaviors or the behaviors related to worship. In this respect, romantic freedom is but another step in this process. Like voting and science itself, the freedom to make intimate romantic choices without a reliance on—or a rigid adherence to—ancient texts (e.g., the Bible) is no less important than divorcing observation and experimentation from ancient authorities too. If thinking on one's own is a moral improvement on ancient texts, the same is no less true about all moral choices, romantic and otherwise. People need to be trusted (unless they violate civil and criminal law), regardless of the weight of purported authorities (religious or otherwise) or hallowed antiquity. Finally, if an independent will is the justification for voting, it is no less a justification for choices we make about romance. Choosing who we love, even on a university campus, is no less a fundamental part of choosing how we live.

Having discussed the meaning of conscience, attention will now be turned to liberty. Since these concepts are used in tandem, one is obviously no less important than the other. If conscience is the internal process by which we make judgments about right and wrong, liberty is the condition that protects it from governmental and institutional interference. The reason and manner by which it is protected is hereby examined.

What is liberty? Or more precisely, how is liberty defined?

Americans are undoubtedly familiar with liberty. A famous statue bears her name. The phrase "life, liberty, and the pursuit of happiness," drawn from the Declaration of Independence, is another case in point. Abraham Lincoln contributed as well, particularly with the opening sentence of his Gettysburg Address: "Four score and seven years ago our fathers brought forth on this continent, a new nation, conceived in Liberty, and dedicated to the proposition that all men are created equal."[17]

Though the word liberty is omnipresent in the archives of U.S. politics, defining it is more difficult than one might anticipate. Americans love liberty and will fight to preserve it, but they are hard-pressed to define it precisely. In this respect they are not alone. Most people simply define liberty as freedom, and vice versa. Though this proves that the words are synonyms and thereby interchangeable, supplemental definitions are obviously needed as well. Does liberty, for instance, give us the freedom to do as we please? Or is liberty limited to protecting us from political oppression? Other questions arise too. Does voting ensure liberty? Or are other guarantees necessary as well?

Berlin, a noted philosopher on this subject, has stated that every moralist in human history has praised the concept of liberty. The same is true for happiness. Moralists inevitably conclude that people should be happy and free. Having said that, two questions arise. What exactly does this mean? And how can it be achieved?

There are unfortunately no easy answers. Where liberty is concerned, difficulties and paradoxes prevail. For example, liberty has been advocated simultaneously with support for slavery, religious prejudice, holy wars, gender discrimination, the destruction of native peoples, and so forth. Does liberty exist, for instance, in the United States, where the land itself was taken from Native Americans? Perhaps liberty is simply a privilege for the privileged? Or alternatively, it can only be achieved at the expense of the loss of liberty to others?

Though ultimately, for the purposes of the discussion here, the primary interest is in how the concept of liberty was conceptualized during the time of the Constitutional Convention, and subsequently formulated within U.S. jurisprudence and the political zeitgeist, it is important, as a first step, to explain what is meant by the term liberty itself. When this is accomplished, it will thereafter be combined with the previous conclusions about conscience, hopefully yielding a meaningful explanation of the phrase liberty of conscience.

In the service of that goal, three different perspectives on liberty will now be introduced: those of Mill (*On Liberty* [1859]), Berlin (*Four Essays on Liberty* [1969]), and Rawls (*A Theory of Justice* [1971]). Though these authors are by no means representative of the field, they are nonetheless being highlighted because they are especially germane to the subject matter of this book: romantic choice.

Take Mill. The general consensus is this: Mill's father, also a prominent philosopher, tutored his brilliant son to great reward. Though highly accomplished as a teenager, Mill unfortunately was also severely depressed by the time he was twenty. Knowledge, perhaps not surprisingly, did not yield happiness. In retrospect, Mill came to view his education as more oppressive than enlightening. When Mill eventually discovered liberty, in both thought and action, his spirits improved. Mill thereafter devoted his life and work to exploring the concept of liberty.

As a first step, Mill asked, What is a valid reason for *interfering* with liberty? His answer was "that the only purpose for which power can be rightfully exercised over any member of a civilized community, against his will, is to prevent harm to others."[18]

The problem, of course, was to define harm. For example, if I lose a race and feel defeated, has the victor harmed me? Or if my shabby clothes make be feel ashamed, did my better-dressed colleagues harm me as well? If contact sports such as football create injuries, should they be banished so as not to create harm to others?

Mill anticipated such concerns and thus fine-tuned what he meant by the term harm. Clearly, there must be harms that are tolerated by society, and those that are not.

Where should the dividing line fall?

Mill concluded that society should only protect its citizens from harms that violate rights. Liberty prevails until someone's rights have been violated.

Is this a reasonable solution? In theory it certainly makes sense. In practice, however, Mill's concept of rights is no less difficult to manage than undistinguished harm. What rights are we talking about, for example?

The American Youth Soccer Organization, for instance, allows every child to make a team and thereafter play soccer. Has liberty prevailed, and have rights been protected? If equal opportunity is at the heart of societal rights, then the answer is yes. The soccer organization has provided access to everyone.

Alternatively, do competitive Division 1 college soccer teams violate liberty and disrespect the rights of potential players who do not qualify? Does failing to make the team and feeling disgruntled signify a violation of rights, much the same as it might signify harm?

Where Mill is concerned, it is difficult to know. What is therefore evident is that rights and harms need to be better clarified in order to fully understand the limits of liberty.

Mill defines liberty itself as "pursuing our own good in our own way." It is a definition that highlights independence ("our own"), happiness ("good"), and choice ("in our own way")—all of which are essential to the experience of liberty. The boundaries of this pursuit are less clear, especially for the present purposes, as they relate to romance.

Though Mill would undoubtedly condemn rape and incest as obvious harms, and would presumably protect nontraditional romantic choices ("in our own way"), establishing clear guidelines for sexual rights is another matter entirely. The limits inherent in Mill's conceptions of societal harms and people's rights make this task extraordinarily difficult.

The spirit of his treatise never disappoints, however. The manner in which Mill justifies the preeminence of liberty, the freedom of choice in particular, and the fact that liberty, not governmental regulation, is the default principle of individual determination (and therefore happiness) can be appreciated and applauded by everyone who values liberty itself.

Perhaps the closest approximation to what the present book considers a useful perspective for conceptualizing liberty can be obtained from the writings Berlin, particularly his "two-concept" point of view: "negative liberty" and "positive liberty."[19]

To put it simply, Berlin indicated that negative liberty was freedom from interference, whereas positive liberty was the freedom of self-determination. They operate conjointly as follows. Liberty exists when you can determine the course of your life without governmental or institutional interference. This is a reasonable, perhaps even admirable, definition of liberty. Controversy arose, though, in the manner in which Berlin hedged his bets.

At least according to Berlin, negative liberty was not the panacea for life's laments. It is instead tempered by concerns for justice, equality, and so forth. Similarly, Berlin was not convinced that positive liberty necessarily flourished in democracy. Civil liberties may exist where democracy prevails, but not necessarily spiritual liberty—the countless discriminations of African Americans being an example that readily comes to mind. The "tyranny of the majority," even in a democracy like the United States, can also be an effective means of crushing minority rights (a whole race of people, in fact), while protecting the civil liberties of others.

Though these issues have been hotly debated, they have yet to be considered in relation to sexual rights. In that domain, they appear, ostensibly at least, to be of vital interest.

One of the foremost concerns with the advocacy of sexual rights is the placement of boundaries. Is there, for example, a constitutional right to engage in prostitution? Is gay marriage similarly protected? Other obvious questions come to mind as well as part of the constitutional debates about sex.[20]

These questions notwithstanding, it is also important to emphasize that sexual choices are always bounded by the notion of harm, specifically tangible harm. Unlike other forms of liberty, sexual liberty immediately raises the question of rape or other types of sexual coercion. Not only is the government capable of oppressing sexual rights; individual citizens routinely sexually oppress each other as well. Rape, sexual harassment, child sexual abuse, and so forth, are notable examples. Sexual liberty is thus ready-made for Berlin's concerns. Namely, at what point is sexual liberty constrained so that it does not constrain the sexual liberty of others? The existence of that constraint is not the matter of debate but instead is limited to where the line is drawn.

Similarly, it is also easy to conceive of a situation where sexual liberties are more likely to flourish under autocratic rule. The tyranny of religious opinion, even in a democracy, is capable of setting strict limits, for example, on the nature of romantic love. Loving, marrying, or having sexual relations with people who are racially different or the same gender have both been outlawed, at one time or another, in the United States alone. It is therefore conceivable that other forms of government, especially those void of a Christian heritage, would permit such unions. But even if this proved untrue, it is still apparent that democracy is no guarantee of sexual rights. Despite the Ninth Amendment, which guarantees the rights retained by the people, the right to make choices about reproduction being a fundamental part, there are still no recognized sexual rights per se in the United States. The people, at best, have a right to privacy—the merits of which are about as useful, I believe, as the term "private parts," which is sufficient nomenclature for a child, but not for an adult.[21]

Finally, we now turn to Rawls for a third perspective. Rawls believes that liberty is best explained by three questions: Who is free? What are they free from? And what are they free to do? Together, they operate as follows. Liberty is evident when a person can act without constraints, and when that person is further protected from external interference.[22]

Protection is once again the key. It is must be legally enforced from two vantage points: the absence of legal restrictions for particular thoughts or actions, in combination with the simultaneous legal duty not to interfere with those particular thoughts or actions. When those conditions are met, liberty, according to Rawls, exists.

Like Berlin, Rawls believes that constraints to liberty nearly always exist. They are necessary, in Rawls's view, in order to gain the benefits of liberty itself. The freedom of speech is a case in point. If all speakers had the liberty to talk whenever they wished and at whatever volume, the merits of free speech would drown in pandemonium. Instead, when rules of order are established, productive speech is more likely to occur.

Rawls also makes a distinction between the existence of liberty and its relative worth. Poverty, for example, can diminish the value of the freedom of speech. When people are destitute, more pressing concerns come to the foreground. While the freedom of speech may continue to have enormous societal merit, it does not invariably serve the needs of the impoverished. Therefore, the capacity to make use of a liberty, according to Rawls, is directly related to its perceived worth.

Returning to the subject matter of this book, it becomes imperative to ask, in the spirit of Rawls, What exactly is romantic liberty on a university campus worth? Compared to starvation, romantic and sexual rights are absurdly trivial concerns. Eating, obviously, takes precedence over making love. But that conclusion notwithstanding, there is a curious connection too. Some of the poorest nations in the world, such as Ethiopia and the Sudan, suffer no less from sexual abuse as from other forms of economic deprivation. For example, the Sudan is infamous for its ritual clitorectomies, a barbaric removal of the clitoris of young girls. Though tolerated under the guise of cultural relativity, much as slavery was tolerated as a culturally entrenched institution, clitorectomy is nothing more than a brutal and ghastly procedure that deprives Sudanese women of their sexual rights in the most primitive fashion known.

Ethiopia is equally notorious for the existence of child prostitutes. Eleven-, twelve-, and thirteen-year-old girls routinely escape poverty through acts of prostitution. Men solicit child prostitutes because of a perceived lowered HIV risk. The end result, unfortunately, is predictable. Young girls eventually contract HIV as well. The intractable problems associated with HIV in Ethiopia and genital mutilation in the Sudan indicate that sexual issues are by no means eliminated by poverty. Instead, it appears that they are exacerbated by it.

The same is perhaps equally true of the freedom of speech. It might be useful to reconsider this issue as well. Though poverty may diminish its value, it may also increase the probability that the freedom of speech will be correspondingly abused. The same reasons that motivate a poor person to ignore the benefits of free speech in exchange for a complimentary meal, make that person equally vulnerable to losing the additional legal counterpart to free speech. Free speech is not worth fighting for if people are distracted by their hunger. Whatever conditions or characteristics create vulnerability undoubtedly create abuse too.

The evaluation of worth is compromised by economic disadvantages. This, however, is merely the perception of worth, not intrinsic worth per se. If, for example, anger and frustration precludes recognizing loving kindness, it does not diminish the intrinsic value of this affection. It merely demonstrates the inability to perceive or appreciate it. The same is arguably no less true of all rights and liberties. Failing to perceive their worth does not diminish their value. Instead, it illustrates the conditions that undermine the perception of their worth.

Three different perspectives on liberty have now been introduced, and each makes a contribution. How, then, should liberty be defined for the present purposes with these perspectives in mind?

The solution, I believe, is to combine them in the following manner. If you are legally entitled to make fundamental choices about your life, and are legally protected from governmental or institutional interference, you have liberty.

Two exceptions warrant comment. If liberty creates a tangible harm, liberty ceases to exist. Or when liberty prohibits the liberty of others, the same is true as well. For example, the harm from sexual coercion eliminates any claim for sexual liberty. There are clearly no legal entitlements to rape. Similarly, if owning beachfront property precludes public access to the beach, the liberty of one person precludes the liberty of others—neither of which can be tolerated by societies that champion liberty for all.

Returning again to the subject matter of this book, it is important in light of the discussion above to once more ask whether professors and students have the liberty to date each other. Or to put it another way, whether adults (in this case, professors and students) are legally entitled to make a fundamental choice about their lives, in the form of a dating relationship, with legal protection from governmental or institutional interference.

The answer should be patently obvious. It is yes, without question. To argue otherwise, it seems to me, is ludicrous in the extreme. Dating is unquestionably a fundamental life choice. Most serious romantic relationships, in fact, begin with a date. It is therefore a necessary prerequisite to the intimate side of life.

Here is another way of looking at this. Presume for the moment that attractions between professors and students were prohibited on college campuses as well. If a professor was physically attracted to a student, they could lose their job. One could make the argument, for instance, that attractions are the preliminary step to dating, making them by association equally detestable too.

It is argued here, however, that it is no less preposterous to prohibit attraction than to deny dating itself. Feeling attracted to someone and thereafter wanting to date them is "nobody's business but my own." Governmental (or institutional) permission should not be required, nor should the government (or powerful institutions) be legally entitled to interfere with such (certainly if such institutions are the recipients of federal funding). This is, or certainly should be, a self-evident truth.

Liberty alone is thus a formidable foundation for protecting romantic and sexual rights. In combination with the concept of conscience, however, it is even more so. Together, as repeatedly asserted throughout this book, they create an extraordinarily powerful platform for securing romantic rights on a college campus. Here is why.

Consider Rawls's position. According to Rawls, the liberties encompassed within one's conscience relate to religious, moral, and philosophical interests. The big question, for this book at least, is whether these interests legitimately relate to romance and sex?

The answer is clearly affirmative, because there are many philosophical perspectives on both romance and sex (Michel Foucault, Plato, etc.), thereby establishing that they are definitely within the purview of philosophy.

Interestingly, religions also provide confirmation. The Bible, for instance, clearly has much to say about romance and sex. The story of Adam and Eve, the commandment about coveting a neighbor's wife, and the immaculate conception are cases in point. Many other examples would similarly suffice.

While it is true that romance and sex have relevance to both religion and philosophy, the present book asserts that romance and sex fit more squarely within our interests about morality. In fact, when morality is debated, it is often about either romance or sex. Examples include debates about premarital sex, abortion, contraception, marriage, homosexuality, adultery, and so forth. The romantic and sexual choices we make are obviously anchored within the domain of conscience, and by extension, protected by the liberty of conscience, unless the choices create tangible harm or deny the liberty of others.

The key word, again, is *protected*. Why is it so important to protect the choices that arise from our conscience? Rawls asserts the following: "[We] can not take chances with [this] liberty by permitting the dominant religious or moral doctrines to persecute or to suppress others if it wishes. Even granting...that it is more probable than not that one will turn out to belong to the majority (if a majority exists), to gamble this way would show that one did not take one's religious or moral convictions seriously, or highly value liberty to examine one's beliefs."[23]

So at least according to Rawls, we scrupulously protect the liberty of conscience because we revere religious and moral convictions to begin with, and we "highly value" the right to examine those beliefs as well.

But here is the paradox. Though religions often condemn ("persecute" or "suppress") a wide range of normative sexual practices (e.g., condom use), a fact implied by Rawls himself, it is our reverence for religion that establishes the liberty to make religious and moral choices based on our conscience in the first place. Religions that promote intolerance, therefore, bite the hand that feeds them. Their very existence, and religious diversity in general, are the distinct beneficiaries of the rights and liberty of conscience—no less so for Williams long ago then for U.S. Christians today.

This point deserves some elaboration, particularly as it relates to the position proposed here. As noted previously, one of the basic components of this argument is that religious freedom is the handmaiden of the rights and liberty of conscience.

Rawls believes instead that it is our reverence for religion that elevates the rights and liberty of conscience. In either case, however, the result is the same. The rights and liberty of conscience, according to both perspectives, is an esteemed and privileged process essential to our personal autonomy.

Which brings up another interesting question. What exactly is a religion? Or for the present purposes, how is religion defined in the Constitution?

Though religious freedom is a mainstay of constitutional dialogue, religion itself is not defined in the Constitution, or for that matter, in the Bill of Rights. This is surprising, given the place of religion in U.S. politics. On the other hand, this is not necessarily a problem if we limit ourselves to the traditional forms of the big five religions: Christianity, Islam, Buddhism, Judaism, and Hinduism. These religions have enough in common to fashion a definition that would unify them all.

Other religions are another matter entirely. This is where the problem arises. Are the belief systems of indigenous people, for example, religions as well? Is atheism a religion? Must a religion have only one God? Or can multiple Gods suffice?

What if there is no God? Can a religion exist without a belief in a supernatural being or beings? If, for example, a group of people has faith in themselves and believes that they are destined to contribute to the world, does that belief and its followers constitute a religion? Why is God, instead of faith, the determining factor?

These questions are significant because the Constitution protects the free exercise of religion. To know exactly what is being protected, it must therefore be defined. Of course, the other alternative is to assert that the rights and liberty of conscience protect all of the relevant belief systems underlying religion. Though this possibility will also be considered later in this chapter and throughout the next, it is still arguably necessary to define religion in the first place.

Besides defining religion, God must also be defined as well. Shinto Gods, for instance, get married and have kids. The Judeo-Christian God, in contrast, is extremely chaste. Are they the same God? Or do their differences require separate God categories.

Other questions also arise. For example, some religions believe that their God is so special that he is the only true God. How, then, are the other Gods defined? Are they lesser Gods? Or are they not Gods at all?

Which brings up another interesting question. When we protect the liberty to believe in God, we are protecting the belief, but not God, because God presumably needs no protection.

What, then, makes this belief so unique? Why, say, is it not necessary to protect the belief in Santa Claus in the same way? Though this question is obviously for argument's sake only, it nonetheless serves a useful purpose.

For instance, God and Santa Claus share much in common. They are widely held beliefs that exist without concrete proof. The difference, of course, is that Santa Claus is an acknowledged fiction, whereas the belief in God, certainly to adherents, is an unverifiable truth.

Yet the big difference between the belief in God and the belief in Santa Claus is the power underlying the belief itself. Unlike Santa Claus, God is worth dying for. Countless millions have died in holy wars. Blood, on the other hand, is rarely shed over Saint Nick.

Why?

Killing for God is justified, or so it seems, because at some level people believe that God appreciates slaughter and revenge. Otherwise, it would seem that people would not kill in God's name.

Nobody presumably kills for Santa Claus. He is the mellower fellow. This is but one distinctive example that makes the belief in Santa Claus extremely different from the belief in God.

Which raises another interesting question. If religion and God have their hand in killing, why do we protect them?

Obviously not all religions, or religions at all times, preach violence. Violence is merely the cancer of fanatic beliefs. We ostensibly protect religion for the good it does, and more important, we protect religions as a consequence of the liberty given to our consciences.

Another motive, however, also comes to mind. Perhaps we protect God and religion in the United States to avoid senseless killing in God's name. Killing for the sake of God or one's religion is so prevalent, even today, that the need for the free exercise of religion, one could argue, is more critical than ever. Giving freedom to every religion should preclude or at the very least reduce the need to fight for any one religion. This suggestion is among the various hypotheses for why religion and the belief in God is protected.

Returning again to the definition of religion from a constitutional point of view, the Supreme Court has also attempted to rectify this dilemma by making its own determinations about what constitutes religion or more precisely a religious practice. The definitive Supreme Court case, curiously, pertained to sex and romantic choice as well—in particular, polygamy.

Though the immaculate conception is a celebrated Christian doctrine, polygamy is not. Reproduction without sex is clearly more preferable than the prospect of simultaneous reproductions.

Polygamy, incidentally, is the practice of having two or more simultaneous wives. In the United States, it was the Mormons in the mid-nineteenth century who embraced this custom. Mormons believed that polygamy was a "religious duty." The rest of Christian America concluded otherwise, branding it as immoral and barbaric.

For example, in a speech before Congress in 1860, U.S. representative John McClernand of Illinois said the following:

As to polygamy, I charge it to be a crying evil, sapping not only the physical constitution of the people practicing it, dwarfing their physical proportions and emasculating their energies, but at the same time perverting the social virtues, and vitiating the morals of its victims.... It is often an adjunct to political despotism; and invariably begets among the people who practice it the extremes of brutal bloodthirstiness or timid and mean prevarication.... It is a scarlet whore. It is a reproach to the Christian civilization; and deserves to be blotted out.[24]

Contrast this point of view with the words of Joseph Smith, founder of the Mormon Church. Polygamy, Smith said, "Is *the* most holy and important doctrine ever revealed to man on the earth."[25] Unfortunately, for polygamous Mormons, it was also a crime in Utah, subsequent to the antipolygamy act of 1862.

The leadership of the Mormon Church in conjunction with the Salt Lake City U.S. attorney decided to resolve their differences by creating a test case to determine whether polygamy, as practiced by Mormons, had constitutional protection.

A volunteer was needed. He would then be arrested under the antipolygamy act. While out on bail, his arrest would be appealed, if necessary, all the way to the Supreme Court. The volunteer was a man named George Reynolds, secretary to Brigham Young. He was also the former editor of the *Millennial Star*.

The manner in which he volunteered is worth noting. As it happened, the second counselor to the president of the Mormon Church walked up to Reynolds on the street and told Reynolds that the first president of the Mormon Church wanted him to be arrested and tried for polygamy. Being a good Mormon, Reynolds agreed on the spot.

Reynolds, as it turned out, was an ideal candidate. Besides being closely connected with Young, he also had more than one wife. Their names were Mary Ann Tuddenham and Amelia Jane Schofield.

The facts of the ensuing trial were as follows. In October 1874, Reynolds was quickly indicted for bigamy. Proving him guilty was much more difficult. Despite fifteen witnesses, Reynolds's father, mother, and the mayor of Salt Lake City (who had married Reynolds to his second wife) among them, nobody seemed to remember enough details to convict him of bigamy. It was not until Schofield admitted, in dramatic testimony, to being Reynolds's second wife that a guilty verdict emerged.

This conviction, however, was overturned shortly after by the territorial Supreme Court. It was determined that the jury, made up of seven Mormons and five non-Mormons, was improperly constituted.

A year later, though, Reynolds was indicted and convicted again. This one proved successful. Reynolds was fined $500 and sentenced to two years imprisonment at hard labor.

Of particular importance in this subsequent trial was Chief Justice Alexander White's charge to the new jury. He stated: "In matters of opinion, and especially in matters of religious belief, all men are free. But parallel with and dominating over this is the obligation which every member of society owes to that society; that is, obedience to the law."[26]

To put this in perspective, White cited further the examples of Hindu mothers and Fiji islanders who kill infants and widows, respectively, for religious reasons. The United States, White asserted, would not tolerate these murders, whatever the religious motive, and it should therefore not tolerate the legal violation of polygamy as well, since the two are presumably comparable. It apparently never occurred to White that murder and reproductive choice were vastly different moral preferences.

The Mormon leadership appealed the Utah court's conviction to the U.S. Supreme Court. On January 6, 1879, Chief Justice Morrison Waite delivered the majority decision in *Reynolds v. the United States*, whereby Reynolds's conviction was upheld.[27]

The Mormon Church was shocked, to say the least. It firmly believed that polygamy had divine inspiration and First Amendment protection. To accept otherwise was contrary to Mormons' fundamental religious beliefs.

The Supreme Court thought differently. Its conclusion provided the foundation for how the United States defines religious practice. At the heart of its decision was the question of "whether religious belief can be accepted as a justification of an overt act made criminal by the law of the land."[28] Like Utah justice White before him, Waite concluded that it could not. While religious beliefs and opinions have the full protection of the First Amendment, actions that violate the law, he insisted, do not.

Unfortunately, the Supreme Court never fully addressed the issue of why polygamy was against the law to begin with, or conversely, whether the liberty of conscience would protect it against criminalization in the first place. Evidence of dysfunctional polygamous marriages or communities, for example, is hardly a good reason for criminalizing polygamy. Such evidence would preclude marriage itself. Furthermore, since polygamy does not create tangible harm, certainly in the form of inherent abuse, or infringe on the liberty of others, it is perhaps an ideal candidate for protection under the rights and liberty of conscience. Meaning that the choice to have more than one spouse, one could argue, is a deeply intimate decision of great enormity to one's existence and family.

Here is another perspective. *Sequential* marriage, subsequent to divorce, is legally protected. It is a practice that is now extraordinarily common in the United States. Many people, in fact, have two or more spouses throughout their lifetime. In contrast, the crime of polygamy is simply the fact that multiple marriages occur simultaneously. If all such marriages, whether simultaneous or sequential, include mutual informed consent among competent adults, and are void of tangible harm (abuse in particular), than neither should be a crime. Or to put it another way, it would be equally unjust to criminalize sequential marriage, asserting that adults were only permitted one spouse per lifetime. Finally, since polygamy, certainly among the Mormons, is clearly a religiously motivated practice, it is arguably the kind of religious practice that needs special protection from the tyranny of the majority. As Jefferson infamously stated many centuries ago: "The rights of conscience we never submitted, we could not submit. We are answerable for them to our God. The legitimate powers of government extend to such acts only as are injurious to others. But it does me no injury for my neighbor to say there are twenty Gods or no God. It neither picks my pocket nor breaks my leg."[29]

Polygamy, it should now be noted, is similar. It challenges conventional morality, but it doesn't pick pockets or break legs. If the Supreme Court needed guidelines for distinguishing religious beliefs and actions that merit First Amendment protection, Jefferson provided as much. Religious sacrifice or murder, as introduced by Justice White above, is an obvious harm far worse than broken legs and thereby rightly criminalized. The question of whom, or how many, to love is another matter entirely.

Taking this a step further, it is also important to note that Jefferson was equally concerned about protecting religious beliefs that run against the grain, even if they proved erroneous, for whatever purpose. "It is error alone which needs the support of government. Truth can stand by itself. Subject opinion to coercion: whom will you make your inquisitors? Fallible men; men governed by bad passions, by private as well as public reasons. And why subject it to coercion? To produce uniformity. But is uniformity of opinion desirable? No more than of face or stature."[30]

The preeminence of Jefferson's opinions notwithstanding, the Supreme Court decided to ignore his definition of harm, and worse yet, coerce Mormons into abolishing their custom of polygamy. Since polygamy was offensive to other Christians, the Supreme Court determined that "being offensive" was a sufficient enough harm to eliminate it among the Mormons.

Justice Waite also maintained that monogamy was essential for democracy, thereby making polygamy antidemocratic—which, of course, means that extramarital affairs are antidemocratic too. In that case, many U.S. presidents and founding fathers were undermining democracy through their nonmonogamy as well. It should also be noted that adultery, like polygamy, is against the law in many states.

Worse yet, Waite drew an analogy between polygamy and the purported practice of wife burning. According to this logic, polygamy is among the most horrific crimes imaginable. Waite concluded: "To permit [polygamy] would be to make the professed doctrines of religious belief superior to the laws of the land."[31]

Though he merely volunteered to act as a test case, Reynolds was nonetheless sent to jail, where he served his term first in Lincoln, Nebraska, and thereafter in Utah.

The usual joke about polygamy is that one is punished by having to live with more than one wife at a time. Reynolds, however, experienced the more conventional punishment in the Big House as well.[32]

Many other Supreme Court decisions about religion obviously followed *Reynolds v. the United States*, including some contemporary cases about the placement of the Ten Commandments. Of particular mention, however, is the case of the *United States v. Ballard*.[33]

The underlying issue was similar to *Reynolds v. the United States*. Though religious beliefs have full protection, the critical question is still, What constitutes a legitimate dividing line between beliefs and religious practices (or actions)? Obviously, communion is a practice, as is a bar mitzvah. But according to *Reynolds*, polygamy is not, because in large part it has been deemed a crime. Now, in *Ballard*, the subject concerned the solicitation of donations based on religious claims of curing disease. The truth of the religious claims and the potential for fraud were also at issue.

The Supreme Court narrowly (five to four) upheld the conviction against Edna and Donald Ballard for soliciting donations based on questionable claims of a cure. What is particularly important to the discussion here, though, is the dissenting opinion of Justice Robert Jackson. Jackson stated:

The chief wrong which false prophets do to their following is not financial. The collections aggregate a tempting total, but individual payments are not ruinous.... But the real harm is on the mental and spiritual plane.... The wrong of these things, as I see it, is not in the money the victims part with half as much as in the mental and spiritual poison they get. But that is precisely the thing the Constitution put beyond the reach of the prosecutor, for the price of freedom of religion or of speech or of the press is that we must put up with, and even pay for, a good deal of rubbish.[34]

Rubbish, like beauty, is in the eye of the beholder. One person's modern sculpture is another person's junk. Or to use Jackson's term, rubbish. What arguably needs to be added to his equation for the present purposes is the acknowledgment that reproductive freedoms and the choices made about romance are accompanied by rubbish (or beauty, as the case may be) as well. Polygamy, homosexuality, faculty-student dating, and so forth, may offend the majority, no less than nontraditional expressions of speech and the press. But as Jackson rightly observes, they are the price we pay for liberty itself. In fact, it is the prevalence of "rubbish" that is the best evidence of the liberty we enjoy. If we truly have the freedom to make choices about love, those choices are bound to offend at least someone—faculty-student romance included. That offense alone (as opposed to tangible harm) is the worst reason to prohibit such unions, particularly in a society that cherishes liberty itself.

One final point deserves mention. The history of the United States is not without grievous harms to liberty, with slavery being but one of the worst examples of its crimes against humanity. The historical absence of liberty is therefore never a persuasive argument for it persisting in the present. This is true for every infringement of the people's rights, including consensual romantic and sexual rights.

That said, it now might be useful to carefully examine exactly what sexual freedoms, broadly conceived, U.S. citizens enjoyed (or at least tolerated) in the formative years of our union. Though such freedoms are not necessarily examples of positive liberty, they are instances of negative liberty—meaning that where sexual freedoms existed, though technically illegal, they nonetheless received considerable protection from governmental interference.

Take all sexual relationships between slaves and their owners. Since slaves did not have the legal capacity for consent, all sexual relationships between slaves and slave owners were coercive. Slaves were also raped and sexually harassed. All sexual relationships between slaves and married slave owners constituted adultery. And so on. The point being that these one-sided, marginal "liberties" persisted despite the crimes they entailed. Southern Christians found a way to tolerate these sexual choices prior to the Civil War, but paradoxically had great difficulty accepting polygamy shortly thereafter.

Prostitution in the nineteenth-century United States is another example. The words of John D'Emilio and Estelle Freedman are especially instructive:

Prostitutes were available to serve the sexual needs of men of every class and ethnic background. Fifty-cent "crib houses" catered to casual laborers who sat on wooden benches waiting for a turn so quick that they barely took down their pants. One- and two-dollar joints might attract young clerks and other white-collar workers. Fancy parlor houses with ornate décor, racy music, and expensive liquor won the loyalty of the more economically privileged.[35]

Though we are accustomed to thinking of prostitution as a crime, it was not until World War I that prostitution was declared illegal throughout most jurisdictions in the United States. Prior to that time, prostitution was a segregated activity, restricted to clearly delineated red-light districts. New

York had the Tenderloin, San Francisco had the Barbary Coast, and New Orleans had Storyville. Even smaller cities had their share of brothels. By the late 1880s, Little Rock, Arkansas, for one, claimed nineteen brothels, while Lancaster, Pennsylvania, boasted twenty-seven.[36]

Female prostitution was tolerated, or so the story goes, on the grounds that it protected good women from male lust. This is hardly a persuasive justification—no more so than contending that heterosexual video pornography, Internet pornography, or dial-a-porn serve the same purpose. Even if the world were populated with sexually wanton women, some men would presumably still procure female prostitutes and masturbate to heterosexual pornography because nonemotional sex appeals to them.

Female prostitution also says more about male sexuality than female chastity. It is testimony to the kinds of sexual choices many heterosexual men prefer to make. The question is whether the liberty of conscience protects those choices too. And of course, whether prostitutes (heterosexual, homosexual, and transgendered) themselves have that liberty as well. Using Jackson's phrase, the ultimate issue becomes, Is prostitution the rubbish we tolerate to ensure the liberty to make sexual and romantic choices in the first place?

Here is one last fact to consider. Besides witnessing the growth of slavery and prostitution, the nineteenth century was also the first time that most states in the United States codified a statutory age of consent. Meaning, simply, that each state specified an age at which someone could legally consent to sex. Guess what age was used?

Ten. (Yes, you read it right. It was ten years of age.)

With this in mind, plus the facts surrounding prostitution and the sexual coercion of slaves, it is disingenuous at best to argue that the history of sexual regulation in the United States has any bearing on judgments made today about sexual rights in this country. If we made ten the legal age of sexual consent, how can we in good conscience deny marriage to same-sex adults or discriminate against coworkers (or faculty and students) who romance each other? If anything, our history is just as much a cautionary tale of what to avoid as a path to enlightenment.

In summation, there is considerable room for improvement where sexual rights are concerned. Taking the meaning and spirit of the rights and liberty of conscience more seriously is an obvious and necessary step in that direction.

In the next chapter, the constitutional history of the rights and liberty of conscience will be considered more fully, chiefly as they relate to the foundation of U.S. jurisprudence in the form of the First and Ninth Amendments. Sexual and romantic rights, in particular, will be woven into this tapestry as becomes relevant. The overall objective is to demonstrate that the steps taken to ensure religious freedom in the United States were designed to ensure the freedoms of conscience more generally, including morality as it relates to consensual romantic choice.

3

Liberty of Conscience and the U.S. Constitutional Archives

To reiterate, the first chapter argued that the rights of conscience are an essential part of our constitutional heritage, are distinct from the freedom of religion, and extend to all matters of substance, sex and romance included, with faculty-student romance being a prototypical example of such.

In the second chapter, the concept of the liberty of conscience was separated into its constituent parts—liberty and conscience—and examined in relation to the perspective proposed within. The separate parts and their combination (the liberty of conscience), it was noted, are all consistent with the manner in which it is being applied to consensual romance. Consideration was also given to the definitions of religion, religious belief, and religious practice, the purpose being to explore their relationship to the rights and liberty of conscience. It was repeatedly asserted that it makes much more sense to posit that the latter heralds the former than its reverse.

In this final chapter, attention is now directed to the use of the term the liberty of conscience (or its corollary, the rights of conscience) in the U.S. constitutional archives, especially those associated with the First and Ninth Amendments. It is, in essence, the final piece of this puzzle. Though other literatures may satisfy the claims made here, perhaps with more authority, the point is that the U.S. constitutional archives can be interpreted as supporting the position taken in this book: that right to make romantic choices is consistent with the manner in which the liberty and rights of conscience were conceived. Though the strength of this interpretation does not rest on this archive or in the manner in which it is now being construed, it is hopefully a logical derivative of such.

There are, of course, many principles that underlie the constitutional archives. The balance of powers is a notable example. Others also come to mind, such as the representative form of government. The big question for this book is whether the rights and liberty of conscience are among them.

As a first step, let us return to the question of religion. Religion plays two roles in the Constitution. The first is historical. The United States was founded in part on the desire for religious freedom. This circumstance created a religiously diverse population, which in turn instilled the virtue of religious toleration.

The second role is necessarily built on the former. When it came time to add the Bill of Rights to the federal Constitution, the first clause of the First Amendment was worded as follows: "Congress shall make no law respecting an establishment of religion, or prohibiting the free exercise thereof."

Amendments and real estate abide by the same rule of significance: "location, location, location." The freedom of religion has the top spot, perhaps signifying its preeminence to both the government and the U.S. populace.

But not every word of this amendment carries the same weight. Three words in particular are far more important than the rest. They are, respectively, known as the *establishment* and *free exercise* clauses.

The question arises about whether they are independent, co-dependent, or contradictory. Though evidence has been offered in support of all three sides, the general consensus is that they are codependent, even if the phrasing implies otherwise.

The Supreme Court uses these clauses to resolve religious issues on an "as needed basis." It is a reasonable strategy because religious questions must be reducible to these two clauses in the first place. The present book, however, takes exception to this interpretation, adding a relevant third clause instead: the rights (or liberty) of conscience.

To date, the Supreme Court has put a substantial amount of time and effort into resolving religious freedom law. Some examples include the following questions: Are there religious exemptions from legal duties? Is the Sabbath on Saturday or Sunday, and do work and employment obligations or restrictions apply on that day? Is school prayer permitted? Are the Ten Commandments religious symbols? Can religious schools or religious instruction receive government funding? And so forth. All of these issues have been hotly contested, reaching to the core of deeply cherished beliefs of many Americans.

There is up to this point perhaps little argument about the role of religion in U.S. jurisprudence. The divergence of opinion occurs instead in the manner of interpretation. The present book has a decidedly different point of view. It resurrects a deleted clause from the First Amendment (or perhaps it borrows a right from the Ninth Amendment), and diverts attention away from both establishment and free exercise, by examining whether the rights (or liberty) of conscience can be expanded to other deeply held beliefs that are not religious in origin or substance. That is the heart of this book, though I want to emphasize once again that the position taken here is that the right to make romantic choices is a fundamental form of expression that is essential to personal autonomy, and by inference liberty itself, regardless of the ultimate scope and meaning of the rights and liberty of conscience. The latter is being offered as a justification of the right to make romantic choices because it is, I believe, consistent with the position I am advocating. If this justification proves to have merit, it might also be useful for the purposes of litigation.

If, for example, the Supreme Court were to follow the interpretations offered here, a shift would undoubtedly occur in the framework of religious and sexual freedoms. Since many cherished rights are now at stake, it is worthwhile to examine the foundation of these differences.

Most legal scholars contend that the First Amendment protects religious opinions and beliefs, but not conduct or actions. This is certainly how the Supreme Court has decided its caseload as well, beginning as noted previously with *Reynolds v. the United States* and the question of the constitutional support for polygamy among Mormons. It is therefore useful to consider Jefferson again because in many respects he is at the heart of this controversy. It was Jefferson, for example, who created the metaphor for the putative boundary between beliefs and conduct.

Two quotes are often pieced together in support of this position. One quote is drawn from Jefferson's "Notes on the State of Virginia," and the other from a letter written to the Danbury Baptist Association. Combined, these quotes purportedly represent both Jefferson's point of view and the original intent behind the First Amendment's religion clauses.

Though these quotes are critical to the issue at hand, the problem is that they have also been, at least according to the present point of view, misinterpreted for over one hundred years. What I hope to demonstrate is that the quotes actually represent the very opposite of the prior interpretations, invalidating almost every judicial decision based on them.

Here, then, are the quotes. Though the first one has been cited in the prior chapter, it is being presented here in a broader context. It will now hopefully provide a better sense of exactly what Jefferson meant.

> The error seems not sufficiently eradicated, that the operations of the mind, as well as the acts of the body, are subject to the coercion of the laws. But our rulers can have authority over such natural rights only as we have submitted to them. The rights of conscience we never submitted, we could not submit. We are answerable for them to our God. The legitimate powers of government extend to such acts only as are injurious to others. But it does me no injury for my neighbour to say there are twenty Gods or no God. It neither picks my pocket nor breaks my leg.[1]

Jefferson, I believe, is saying the following. The law has the capacity to coerce operations of the mind and acts of the body. In our country, however, rulers were not given authority over natural rights. (Natural rights, incidentally, include beliefs and conduct—the freedom from slavery being an obvious example of the latter.) This is particularly true where the rights of conscience are concerned (meaning the freedoms to think, choose, and judge). Such rights could not be submitted to the government in the first place since they are relevant only to the covenant between God and the believer. (This position is also consistent with the notion of a limited form of government.) Finally, the government has jurisdiction only over acts that injure others, such as stealing from someone or breaking legs.

The bottom line is this. Beliefs and conduct are protected from government intrusion. This is especially true if they are relevant to natural rights, with the rights of conscience being a preeminent example. Furthermore, the government can only intervene when conduct is injuring someone else, such as theft and bodily harm.

Now before turning to the second quote, it is important to understand that the Supreme Court and countless legal scholars have paradoxically used this second quote to deny First Amendment protection for all conduct, whether injurious or not, even if stemming from the rights of conscience. Beliefs and opinions alone have been deemed suitable for First Amendment protection.

How did this turn of events occur? And how could this conclusion persist in light of Jefferson's opinion, quoted above, in the first place?

Before answering these questions, Jefferson's entire letter to the Danbury Baptist Association is presented below:

Gentlemen, the affectionate sentiments of esteem and approbation which you are so good as to express towards me, on behalf of the Danbury Baptist Association, give me the highest satisfaction. My duties dictate a faithful and zealous pursuit of the interests of my constituents, and in proportion as they are persuaded of my fidelity to those duties, the discharge of them becomes more and more pleasing.

Believing with you that religion is a matter which lies solely between man and his God, that he owes account to none other for his faith and his worship, that the legislative powers of government reach actions only, and not opinions, I contemplate with sovereign reverence that act of the whole American people which declared that their legislature should "make no law respecting the establishment of religion, or prohibiting the free exercise thereof" thus building a wall of separation between church and State. Adhering to this expression of the supreme will of the nation in behalf of the rights of conscience, I shall see with sincere satisfaction the progress of those sentiments which tend to restore to man all his natural rights, convinced he has no natural right in opposition to social duties.

I reciprocate your kind prayers for the protection and blessing of the common Father and Creator of man, and render to you for yourselves and your religious association, assurances of my high respect and esteem.[2]

Four key phrases warrant immediate attention. They are: "the legislative powers of government reach actions only"; "thus building a wall of separation between church and State"; "in behalf of the rights of conscience"; and finally, "restore to man all his natural rights."

Before considering these phrases in depth, it is important to emphasize the following. Most of the limitations placed on behaviors associated with the freedom of religion are derived from only one of these phrases—"the legislative powers of government reach actions only." Over and over again, legal scholars and Supreme Court justices quote this phrase as justification for concluding that the Constitution only protects religious beliefs, but not religiously motivated actions. This conclusion is regrettable.

To begin with, it is disappointing to discover that for over one hundred years, Supreme Court justices never asked the simple question, What *actions* is Jefferson talking about? Is it, for example, all actions, or perhaps some fraction of them?

The answer is obvious. Jefferson, in fact, answered it himself. Furthermore, it is an answer that was also well-known to Supreme Court justices (and all the associated legal scholars too). It is actions that injure others that represent the legitimate use of legislative powers. *Injure* is the determining factor. Like breaking a leg.

To claim otherwise is selective reporting at best, and misstates the remainder of the Danbury Baptist letter as well. Natural rights and the rights of conscience, for instance, refer to both conduct and opinions—the "pursuit of happiness" being a case in point. It would be absurd to argue that pursuing happiness is limited to only beliefs and opinions. Actions as well as beliefs are obviously necessary for implementing this right—sending a congratulatory e-mail to a friend being among the countless examples of such. Consequently, Jefferson's letter continues to extol the merits of both of these (actions and beliefs) too.

Finally, the "separation of church and state" creates a boundary between religion and government, divesting control of the former over the latter (and vice versus). As the letter attests, however, it has no direct relevance to the question of whether the freedom of religion protects opinions, conduct, or both.

Clearly, the Supreme Court has made a mistake.

Here is another way of looking at this. If in the first quote Jefferson used different examples of injury, such as "made me angry and upset," one could argue that his concept of injury included psychological harm. In that case, one could deny polygamy on the grounds that it upsets people.

But Jefferson did just the opposite. He used examples of tangible harm, such as theft and broken bones. Polygamy, as noted in the previous chapter, produces neither consequence.

Moreover, as argued above, Jefferson never meant all actions. The government could only intervene with actions that had the capacity to create tangible harm. Intervention is therefore legitimate only when tangible harm exists.

Here is another problem to consider. Presume for the moment that sending a valentine and stabbing someone through the heart are both religiously motivated behaviors. The manner in which the Supreme Court has consistently misinterpreted Jefferson makes these two actions, at least theoretically, equally deserving of First Amendment prohibition.

This is nonsensical, of course. Yet when Jefferson's concept of injury is added to the mix, the conundrum is resolved. The government has a legitimate interest in prohibiting (and punishing) injurious behavior (e.g., shooting in the heart), but has no standing in prohibiting a behavior born from the right (or liberty) of conscience (e.g., sending a valentine).

In summation, this book differs from the opinions of its predecessors, at least on this point, because it asserts that there has been a fundamental error in interpreting Jefferson. Adding the word injurious to the concept of actions is the key distinction, no less so as it relates to love (e.g., faculty-student romance) and sex (e.g., polygamy). If the government were prohibited from intervening from all beliefs and noninjurious actions, there would be much less of a necessity for this book. Or so one would hope.

Before proceeding further, a word of caution is necessary. There are undoubtedly as many problems with as there are obvious benefits to the use of the archival records that surround the Constitution and its framers. The ostensible benefit is that the records provide insight into motives and intent. Problems also arise where interpretation is concerned, particularly with attempting to interpret writings that are at least two hundred years old.

Besides the potential for misinterpretation, the record is often annoyingly incomplete or directly contradicts itself. The framers, for example, often have vastly different memories of the same event, or have discrepant motives in the first place. Worse yet, there are occasions where framers appear to contradict themselves—Jefferson included.

As noted above, Jefferson makes it clear in his "Notes on the State of Virginia" that the government can only intervene when actions are injurious. Jefferson makes a similar point in his Bill of Religious Freedom: "That it is time enough for the rightful purposes of civil government for its officers to interfere when principles break out into overt acts against peace and good order."[3]

The question is whether "against peace and good order" is synonymous with "injurious." If war or unrest is a threat to peace, the answer is yes. Actions that obviously disrupt peace are injurious as well.

But can the same be said of "good order"? The phrase, unfortunately, is sufficiently vague to argue it both ways. For instance, perhaps Jefferson used "good order" merely as a synonym for "peace"—as in, disturbing the peace disrupts good order. Or conversely, maybe Jefferson meant "good order" as a moral judgment, the violation of which disrupts the good order of society.

In light of Jefferson's own views on religion and morality, it is hard to conceive of the latter interpretation. Yet the Supreme Court in *Reynolds v. the United States* concluded otherwise. It prohibited polygamy because it disrupts the good order of monogamy and more generally morality.

The question then becomes, Did Jefferson contradict himself?

Presume for a moment that a contradiction occurred. The question is not which side to take but instead how to resolve the contradiction itself. For the present purposes, the resolution is simple. Prohibiting actions that are injurious is a much more legitimate purpose of government (and quasi-governmental institutions, such as universities) than prohibiting actions that disrupt a particular moral point of view. The rights and liberty of conscience, as repeatedly asserted, also protect the latter.

In support of this position, the constitutional history surrounding the rights (and liberty) of conscience itself will now be examined.

Conscience versus Religion

Though this history often begins with the federal Constitution, it should also include the history of state constitutions as well. Exploring the Articles of Confederation, and other relevant correspondence and literatures, makes this exercise even more comprehensive. This is particularly necessary where the rights and liberty of conscience are concerned, because the concepts are ever present and constantly changing.

For example, when Madison first proposed an amendment to the Constitution (in the House of Representatives on June 8, 1789) that would protect the freedom of religion, he drafted it as follows: "The civil rights of none shall be abridged on account of religious belief or worship, nor shall any national religion be established, nor shall the full and equal rights of conscience be in any manner, or on any pretext infringed."[4]

Since the rights of conscience are presented in a separate clause, which incidentally does not mention the word religion, it seems reasonable to conclude that at least according to Madison, the rights of conscience are not limited to religion alone.

Samuel Livermore's subsequent motion (in the House of Representatives on August 15, 1789) is consistent with this conclusion. Livermore suggested that the amendment be altered to express the following: "That congress shall make no laws touching religion, or infringing the rights of conscience."[5] Presumably, if the rights of conscience were synonymous with or subsumed by religion, the second clause would be redundant with the first.

Five days later (August 20, 1789), Fisher Ames of Massachusetts made a motion in the House of Representatives for yet another change in this amendment. His suggestions were as follows: "Congress shall make no law establishing religion, or to prevent the free exercise thereof, or to infringe the right of conscience."[6]

And so it stayed, until this amendment went to the Senate on August 25, 1789, where it was continuously revised as well. At first the changes were minor, in large part resembling the suggestion by Ames. Eventually, however, the phrase "rights of conscience" was dropped from its wording entirely.

The House of Representatives was not satisfied with the Senate version, though. A joint committee of members from both Houses (Madison among them) thereafter drafted the amendment as it is known today. Notably missing from the amendment is any reference to either the liberty or rights of conscience.

The big question—certainly as it relates to the present argument—is, why the change?

Michael McConnell asserts that the phrase "rights of (or liberty of) conscience" was dropped from the First Amendment in order to ensure that constitutional protection would not be extended to secular claims of conscience.[7] The conscience buck, in the secular sense, stops right here.

Though this conclusion is quite different from the one proposed here, there is most certainly archival support for McConnell's position as well. Even though no notes exist from the committee that actually drafted the amendment, several other documents make it clear that the rights of conscience was often used solely in reference to religion. State proposals, for example, for a freedom of religion amendment often used the words in tandem. New York's proposal stated the following (July 26, 1788): "That the people have an equal, natural and unalienable right, freely and peaceably to Exercise their

Religion according to the dictates of Conscience."[8] North Carolina and Rhode Island issued proposals with similar wording.

Also, many of the state charters and constitutions placed the word conscience firmly within religion. The Charter of Delaware (1701), for instance, stated: "1. Because no people can be truly happy, though under the greatest enjoyment of civil liberties. If abridged of their freedom of their consciences, as to their religious profession and worship."[9]

Other examples could be cited as well, lending credence to McConnell's conclusion.

But here is the curious part. In many other instances, the rights of conscience are clearly separated from explicit reference to the freedoms of religion. Take the Massachusetts proposal (February 6, 1788): "That the Constitution be never construed to authorize Congress to infringe upon the just liberty of the press, or the rights of conscience."[10] Or the one from New Hampshire (June 21, 1788): "Congress shall make no laws touching religion, or to infringe the rights of conscience."[11] Finally, the constitution of New Hampshire (1783) is particularly instructive: "[Part I, Article] IV. Among the natural rights, some are in their very nature unalienable, because no equivalent can be given or received for them. Of this kind are the RIGHTS OF CONSCIENCE."[12]

So what is ultimately true about this debate is that there is evidence in the constitutional archives to support both claims. The rights of conscience are solely embedded in religious freedom, as suggested by McConnell, and the two concepts are clearly independent, as argued in this book.

The language of the First Amendment is equally indecisive. Although the rights of conscience was clearly dropped from earlier versions of this amendment, suggesting once again that the phrases are redundant, two other reasonable interpretations exist as well. The first is the fact that some of the framers of the Constitution thought the rights of conscience to be independent of religious freedom, and therefore insisted on including it in the amendment in the first place.

Second, just because it was dropped from the First Amendment does not necessarily mean that it was considered redundant. Equally feasible is the hypothesis that the framers, in the spirit of compromise, felt that it was protected by another amendment entirely—the Ninth Amendment in particular—and left it to reside there. The rights of conscience, which are clearly natural (inalienable) rights, thereby became yet another right not enumerated but nevertheless still retained by the people, making the Ninth Amendment a suitable home for them.

Here are the facts that are consistent with this interpretation. As indicated above, Madison wrote the amendment in the first place, when it included the separate phrase "rights of conscience." Madison was also a member of the joint committee that revised it into its present form. It seems reasonable, at least to me, to cautiously conclude that as a compromise, Madison transferred this right to another amendment he authored—namely, the Ninth Amendment, which states: "The enumeration in the Constitution of certain rights, shall not be construed to deny or disparage others retained by the people."

Clearly, Madison did not need to enumerate every right—natural rights in particular—that he considered important, because the Ninth Amendment was his safety net. In order to manage the compromise of the First Amendment, which protects many other freedoms (religion, the press, speech, and peaceable assembly), Madison might simply have offered to shift this additional freedom to the Ninth Amendment's multiple rights.

Finally, as emphasized in the first chapter, Madison clearly envisioned two forms of the liberty of conscience. One, in particular, protects our natural rights to think, judge, and choose. In many respects this sounds more appropriately assigned to the Ninth Amendment, since it relates to a series of broadly encompassing natural rights and underlies the process (and thereby the exercise) of the liberty of conscience.

Is this a plausible scenario? Consider the following.

The Ninth Amendment was sent to the Senate on the same day as the First Amendment (August 25, 1789), and the agreed on and enrolled resolutions of both amendments occurred on the same days as well (September 25 and 28, 1789, respectively). This is by no means proof of the interpretation proposed here but is instead at the very least consistent with this hypothesis.

Here is another way of looking at this. Madison conceived of the Ninth Amendment as protecting natural rights, a designation that was often applied to the rights of conscience. It therefore seems just as reasonable to again conclude that the rights of conscience, so labeled a natural right, found a "better and broader" home in Madison's Ninth Amendment, as to abide by McConnell's belief that it was jettisoned for being redundant with religious freedom.

What, then, do we make of the two different perspectives? If the documentary evidence appears to support McConnell's interpretation just as readily as the one presented here, how do we resolve this conundrum?

Perhaps the First Amendment can be of assistance here as well, especially the establishment clause. The purpose of this clause is twofold. It is designed to prohibit the establishment of a national religion as well as *preference* among the various religions. It is the latter meaning that is important here.

When Supreme Court justices and their corresponding legal scholars denied the rights (and liberty) of conscience for secular as opposed to religious reasons (e.g., for resisting military service), they felt justified in this interpretation because of the supporting archival materials. Unfortunately, as indicated above, this interpretation rests on a selected reading of those resources.

There is, as also noted previously, an equally sufficient documentary record to support the contrary position. The rights of conscience, certainly according to Madison, are part of the foundation of the natural rights of humanity, giving them just as much standing for secular issues too. In essence, what the Supreme Court has done is to give preference to one interpretation over the other.

What makes this particularly distressing is that the Supreme Court has chosen to prefer the exclusively religious interpretation to the more expansive natural rights approach, thereby discriminating against those whose deeply held beliefs are not directly tied to religious metaphors. There are people, many in fact, who contribute vastly to our culture, but do not believe in God or profess any religion. They, too, are entitled to follow the dictates of their conscience, without taking a subordinate status to those who believe otherwise. The failure to acknowledge their rights of conscience is, I believe, tantamount to preferring the religious to the nonreligious. Jefferson felt that it did not matter whether someone believed in twenty Gods or none. The Constitution supports the same view.

It is perhaps now worth considering the relevance of two documents as they relate to the issues raised above: Madison's "Memorial and Remonstrance against Religious Assessments" (June 20, 1785) and the Virginia Bill for Religious Freedom of 1786 (originally authored by Jefferson).

Here are two perspectives arguing against religious preference. Though these protests are not about the rights of conscience per se but instead about a bill requiring contributions to be used for Christian teachers, they nonetheless go to the heart of the matter—that is, the reasons we do not create a preference for religion. Both documents make the same points with equal force.

For example, the Virginia Bill for Religious Freedom states the following: "That to compel a man to furnish contributions of money for the propagation of opinions which he disbelieves, is sinful and tyrannical.... [T]hat our civil rights have no dependence on our religious opinions, more than our opinions in physics and geometry."[13]

These two sentences are incomprehensible without acknowledging a separation between the rights of conscience and the freedom of religion. It is, as stated, both tyranny and a sin to compel a person to furnish money for a religious idea one doesn't believe in. Furthermore, the protection of that person's civil rights is also not dependent on their beliefs about religion, physics, or geometry. An individual's rights of conscience must be upheld regardless of their religious beliefs.

Madison's comments are perhaps even more forceful than these and provide an even stronger foundation for the separation of religious freedom from the rights of conscience. Two phrases, in particular, warrant careful consideration. The first is as follows:

The preservation of a free government requires, not merely that the metes and bounds which separate each department of power may be invariably maintained, but more especially, that neither of them be suffered to overleap the great barrier which defends the rights of the people. The rulers who are guilty of such an encroachment, exceed the commission from which they derive their authority, and are tyrants. The people who submit to it are governed by laws made neither by themselves, nor by an authority derived from them, and are slaves.[14]

Though, as Jefferson advised, there may be a wall separating church from state, and the three branches of the government from each other, neither is as strong, at least according to Madison, as the "great barrier" that defends the rights of people, including the rights of conscience (and for that matter, sexual and romantic rights too). Similarly, if governments encroach on those rights, they are tyrants. Worse yet, people who submit to them are slaves.

Which brings us back to the issue at the heart of this book: the choice of whom to romance. It is without question one of the quintessential rights retained by the people. When a governing body or institution (with considerable federal funding) denies this right to consenting adults, or worse, takes their job away for exercising this right, it is in my view acting the part of the tyrant. There is no reason to mince words here.

But the interesting implication, raised by Madison himself, is that those who accept such situations are acting the part of the slave. This is not particularly flattering either. Both the tyrant and the slave therefore need to acknowledge their complicity in this unholy union.

The second phrase of significance in Madison's essay is this: "Whilst we assert for ourselves a freedom to embrace, to profess and to observe the religion which we believe to be of divine origin, we cannot deny an equal freedom to those, whose minds have not yet yielded to the evidence which has convinced us."[15]

Clearly, then, the unconvinced are destined to enjoy the same freedoms as the religiously confirmed, once again suggesting that the rights of conscience are, in Madison's mind, not limited to the religiously inclined.

This is not to say that the documentary evidence is crystal clear on this matter. The opposite, as repeated above, is true. There is evidence to support both sides. The main problem, instead, is the manner of resolution. To deny the rights of conscience for secular beliefs gives clear preference to those who "profess and observe" religion. That clearly violates Madison's intention and is ultimately contrary to the basic principles underlying the Bill of Rights in the first place.

Which brings us to the second issue that distinguishes the argument proposed in this book from all others: the premise that the rights (and liberty) of conscience protect morality in general, but more important, extend this benefit to opinions and conduct related to consensual romance and sex. This interpretation is by no means popular, which in and of itself is not a condemnation. Many cherished freedoms—against racial discrimination, for example—were highly unpopular at some point in our history.

Here is the problem. If the Supreme Court has been reluctant to extend these protections to secular conduct per se, it is certainly at present unlikely to be persuaded to extend these protections to consensual romance and sex as well. Yet this is no justification for silence. As Madison noted over two hundred years ago, when we accept the encroachment of our rights, we act the part of slaves. This book is meant to challenge that status and break, at least symbolically, those chains.

Conscience and Romantic Choice

There is, unfortunately, nothing in the constitutional archives that makes specific reference to romance or sex. The Constitution is also equally silent on these matters. Nor is there any documentary evidence placing romance or sex within the rights of conscience. The paper trail, relevant to the arguments presented here, leads unfailingly to a dead end.

On the other hand, the constitutional archives are notoriously incomplete. It therefore comes as no surprise that the topics of romance and sex were absent from public debate. This does not mean that romance and sex were irrelevant, however. In fact, it is hard to imagine that romance, or certainly sex, is ever far from the minds of men, including those who framed the Constitution.

There are, of course, many other topics that are absent from constitutional consideration as well. For example, eating and bodily elimination both fall into this category. The big question, then, is what to make of this. Does the absence of attention translate into the absence of protection? Or perhaps one could contend that these three functions (eating, eliminating, and procreating) are so necessary to species survival that there has never been a need to debate them.

Bodily elimination, for instance, is a nondiscretionary activity, even though the time and place can certainly be regulated. The same is true of eating. Yet if both are prohibited, the individual and the species will not survive.

Sex, however, is slightly different. If it is prohibited, the individual can survive, but not the species. Thus, at some level, all three are necessary for species survival and need protection in order to perpetuate the population of the United States, before ever considering the freedoms of religion, speech, and the press.

Of course where sex is concerned, one could also assert that the existence of criminal law makes the deficits in constitutional law less significant. It is perhaps not as important to protect sexual rights if sexual violations are vigorously prosecuted instead. The opposite is much more likely to be true, though.

The criminalization of sexual behavior makes it more imperative to establish the territory of sexual rights beforehand.

If sexual rights (as well as those of romance) are not firmly established to begin with, it becomes extraordinarily difficult to prevent governments from trampling those rights through its power to criminalize a sexual act whenever it becomes convenient to do so, particularly if the act contradicts a prevailing religious belief. Religious institutions throughout history have campaigned to create laws that match their religious objectives. Taxing the general public during the postrevolutionary period to provide funds for Christian teachers is one case in point. One could also argue that the laws prohibiting same-sex marriage are similarly motivated. Both are designed to promote a Christian point of view. Therefore, although the constitutional archives may be silent about sex, there is no reason to believe that sex should be similarly muted. The species cannot survive without sex, and the pursuit of happiness, a cherished U.S. right in and of itself, is also intimately dependent on it (as it is with love and romance). Sexual rights, broadly conceived, thereby need strong protection for the greater good of humanity.

Finally, the criminalization of sex also makes it imperative to establish a strong constitutional footing for sexual rights to ensure that the division between the two is reasonably apparent. The Ninth Amendment, without question, is the best place to start. The present book extends this logic by demonstrating the Ninth Amendment's relevance to the rights (and liberty) of conscience. This obviously includes sex, but more important, it also includes the larger moral questions that underlie our sexual choices themselves.

Returning to the task at hand, the applicable literatures will now be reviewed to see if a case can still be made for placing

sexual and romantic rights within the rights of conscience—
even when the constitutional archive itself fails to do so. As a
first step in the service of that goal, the words of Madison will
be examined once again.

Madison's presidential inaugural address is a good place to
start. It provides, yet again, strong evidence that Madison
made a clear distinction between three types of interrelated
rights: those retained by the people, the rights of conscience,
and finally religion. These differences are crucial in demonstrating that both the people's rights and the rights of conscience were conceived as existing beyond the traditional
confines of religion.

Describing the many goals of his presidency, Madison promised, among other things, "to respect the rights and authorities
reserved to the States and to the people as equally incorporated
with and essential to the success of the general system; to avoid
the slightest interference with the rights of conscience or the
functions of religion, so wisely exempted from civil jurisdiction."[16]

Here, then, is part of the foundation for arguing that both
the Ninth Amendment and the rights of conscience protect essential rights, among which, it is asserted, are romantic and
sexual rights, most notably including the choice of whom to
romance. For example, at least according to Madison, who
was both the architect of the Constitution and the creator of
the Bill of Rights, the rights reserved to the people have equal
standing with all other rights and powers, and furthermore,
that such rights are "essential to the success of the general system." This much Madison makes perfectly clear. It means that
the rights retained by the people deserve the same respect and
protection as everything else. Moreover, if this should fail, the
whole system goes asunder.

Are romantic rights legitimate "rights retained by the people"? Here are three ways of looking at this. First, as discussed in a previous book of mine (*Sexual Rights in America*), it is constructive to reduce this question to whether "the people" have the "right to reproduce." If the answer is yes, which it could not be otherwise, this right is best described as the choice of whether to reproduce or not. Merely being given the mandate to reproduce is not a right but instead governmentally proscribed reproduction. Having the choice to reproduce, on the other hand, gives everyone the right to make autonomous decisions about the most intimate aspect of life. Thus, it is inconceivable that the people do not have the right to make choices about reproduction, which protects as well the choice of sexual partners (e.g., romance) in addition to the devices (e.g., contraception) and behaviors (e.g., oral sex) that might prohibit reproduction. Without such further protections, the choice to reproduce becomes vacuous because in essence it eliminates the choice.

Since the people obviously have the right to make choices about reproduction and the partners with whom to reproduce, that right has the same force as every other right reserved to the people, meaning that it must be respected equal to all other rights and powers, with the understanding that such protection is essential to the integrity of the entire system. The United States stands and falls on sexual and romantic rights no less than the freedoms of speech and the press.

If sexual and romantic rights are protected within the grand scheme of the rights retained by the people, why additionally conceptualize them as a Ninth Amendment right of conscience?

The answer, simply, is that it provides additional protection (much like due process strengthens an argument). More important, it elevates the underlying process, making it clear that sexual and romantic choices, love being a preeminent example, are among the most intimate, conscientious choices we make, parallel for many people with the choices made about religion. Whom to romance can be just as powerful as what one believes.

The history of U.S. jurisprudence also suggests that sexual rights are among the least protected personal rights. Even to this day, most legal scholars still persist in maintaining that sexuality rights per se do not exist but instead achieve some measure of protection under the right of privacy. This book, in contrast, asserts the opposite. Sexual rights (including romantic rights) have always existed within the constitutional schema, under both the Ninth Amendment's rights retained by the people (e.g., the right to reproduce) and the implied First Amendment's rights (and liberty) of conscience. Adding the rights of conscience to this list has both practical and theoretical significance: practical in the sense that it adds another tier of protection, and theoretical in the sense that it provides yet another persuasive rationale for constitutional support.

One could also argue, however, that the protections provided by the Ninth Amendment and the rights of conscience are redundant, since the one is subsumed in the other. Though perhaps this is true, the distinction between the two is still noteworthy because the Ninth Amendment signifies the relevant category for sexual rights (i.e., natural rights), while the rights of conscience justifies the process whereby sexual and romantic rights are given the same standing as other deeply felt, and personally defining, beliefs and actions—morality among them. Sex, like love and romance, makes the world go around, including in the ivory tower.

Second, as also emphasized previously, the framers often made choices in their personal lives that suggest that they too believed that sexual and romantic rights were rights retained by the people. The evidence, as discussed below (and introduced in the first chapter), will clearly demonstrate that the framers' sexual and romantic choices were not a matter of impulse but instead done with careful deliberation, making them ostensibly choices of conscience on the same order—or worse, I believe—as the romantic and sexual choices made on college campuses today. In that respect, these choices are no different than the profound, and often difficult, decisions that are made about God and religion as well.

Take Jefferson. Here is a man who in his mid-forties fell in love with a young girl, named Sally Hemings, who was somewhere between fifteen and eighteen years of age. Sally, incidentally, was also Jefferson's slave.

What makes this romance particularly interesting is that it occurred in Paris. Though a slave in the United States, Sally was a free young woman in France. As the story goes, Jefferson promised Sally that all of her children would be liberated if she returned to the United States with him. Sally consented, and thereafter they had six children together.[17]

While often decried as sordid and elicit, this story is arguably romantic as well. It is, for example, the tale of a prominent and perhaps lonely widower who recaptures his youth after falling in love (or perhaps lust, or both) with a beautiful mixed-race young woman in the enchanting city of Paris. Their infatuation blossoms, persists over two continents, and despite their profound differences (in race, age, status, etc.), culminates in a large family.

Although the fairy-tale version of this union is no less questionable than every other account, all versions minimally provide testimony to the duration of the relationship—meaning that it clearly lasted a long time. Jefferson therefore had ample opportunity to reflect on his choices, including his decision to initiate the relationship, continue it in France as well as the United States, and have many children (implying other choices about contraception and sexual activity too). All of this suggests that he continuously exercised his rights of conscience therein.

Madison fell in love with an equally young partner (approximately fifteen years of age) when he was in his thirties, though unlike Jefferson, his efforts were ultimately dashed when she chose a younger man instead. Yet Madison's motives were apparently sexual, despite whatever other interests he professed to have had in this very young lady. Their age discrepancy alone suggests as much. Furthermore, his choice to pursue this relationship was deliberate and thoroughly considered, once again indicating a choice of conscience.

Similarly, his marriage to the widow Dolly Madison is distinctive as well. It remained childless, suggesting perhaps infertility on his part (Dolly had children previously) or a joint decision of conscience to practice infertile sex (or no sex at all). Other illustrious examples also exist, including the extramarital affair of Alexander Hamilton, and Ben Franklin's penchant for prostitutes. The framers often made curious sexual and romantic choices, suggesting that they gave themselves the right to consider as well as act on those choices.

Finally, to reiterate a theme introduced above, it needs to be stressed that for many people, the choices they make about their intimate relationships, sex and romance included, carry as much meaning, commitment, and force as those they make about their religion and God. The power of a romantic relationship, in fact, is often experienced as "divine," and it is pursued and cultivated with as much passion, if not more so, than many people invest into their religious beliefs. This power alone, plus the time and attention given to the deliberations about such, including the wisdom about the intimate relationship itself (hence, a question of morality), is testimony to the extent to which people consult their consciences when making choices about sex and romance. The importance of distinguishing right from wrong has as much bearing on romance and sex as on any other part of life. If the conscience is the seat of this process, it belongs no less to sex and romance than to religion.

This, ultimately, is the rationale for protecting romantic choice on a college campus. In my view, the logic of such is also more important than the specific legal arguments offered herein.

Returning once again to the founders, it is often difficult to think of them exercising romantic and sexual rights, perhaps confusing the image of a Puritan with a postrevolutionary American. It thus might also be useful to complete this picture by examining the sexual mores of the eighteenth century. Philadelphia in the late 1700s is an ideal place for scrutiny because it was the site of the Constitutional Convention and the original seat of the federal government.

Here is how Richard Godbeer describes the city during the mid-eighteenth century:

The sexual climate in Philadelphia was remarkable for its lack of restraint. Casual sex, unmarried relationships, and adulterous affairs were commonplace, much to the dismay of more straitlaced residents who held that sex should not occur outside of marriage. The city swarmed with young women and men who had migrated there in search of work.... Most of these young people had come to Philadelphia on their own and found themselves free to act pretty much as they pleased. The constant flow of people in and out of the city combined with the greater anonymity of urban life to facilitate casual encounters and informal liaisons ... there was comparatively little pressure upon the city's unmarried inhabitants to think of sexual involvement as a component of courtship; if lovers conceived a child, they were much less likely to marry.... Meanwhile, husbands and wives inclined to cheat on their spouses found ample opportunity to do so....

The city's most notorious symbols of disorder and sexual license were taverns and whorehouses.... Brothels were in plentiful supply and seem to have done a roaring trade.... [B]awdy houses were scattered across the city and frequented by men from every walk of life.[18]

Clearly, then, the sexual climate that prevailed at that time and place, and surrounded the Constitutional Convention itself, was hardly chaste. The opposite appears true in fact. Two of the framers of the Constitution (Franklin and Hamilton) indulged in this sexual cornucopia, and there is no reason to believe that others did not as well.

The question is whether such individuals believed that they had the right to do so, and whether they consulted their consciences about such choices, particularly as it reflected on their moral judgments and those of their other family members.

Given the power of sex and romance to touch so many aspects of one's life—from happiness to children—it seems highly unlikely that romantic decisions were not seriously reflected on, especially within the confines of one's conscience. If so, it would place these choices within the scope of the rights of conscience, ultimately making them no less protected (even if transferred to the Ninth Amendment) than those made about religion.

Of course, this does not mean that every romantic choice is equally protected, or for that matter, that every religious choice is equally protected. Actions that create tangible harm or prohibit the liberty of others are universally condemned and prohibited. Otherwise, the rights of conscience prevail, and as Madison noted, are so wisely exempted from civil jurisdiction.

Finally, it should also be mentioned that religion, no less than sex, was also conspicuously missing from the debates incorporated within the Constitutional Convention. Though religion certainly emerged in the Bill of Rights, it is important to stress that it was absent from the debates that preceded it. The standard story holds that religion was excluded from the constitutional debates because it wasn't one of the underlying principles inherent in the Constitution itself. More likely, however, is that religion would create controversy, which would disrupt the debates, create dissension, and foil the overall effort to gain a unified federal constitution. In support of this conclusion is the evidence that indicates that other "nonprincipled" issues came under scrutiny, despite the absence of religion. When the question of the proper powers of the general legislature was discussed, for example, the following suggestion was voiced: "To establish seminaries for the promotion of literature and the arts and sciences."[19]

Note that the subject of religion is conspicuously missing. On the other hand, a subsequent motion was also made that "no religious test or qualification shall ever be annexed to any oath of office under the authority of the U.S."[20]

Although religion certainly made its appearance in the Bill of Rights, it was apparently not essential to the Constitution itself. The opposite appears to be true; care was taken to ensure that it did not relate to an oath of office.

Lastly, though the fact that sex and romance were left out of constitutional dialogue can be lamented, they are without question nobler causes than at least one issue that made it in: namely, slavery. Often riled for the sexual crimes it perpetuated, and despite its violation of the lofty rhetoric of the Constitution and the Bill of Rights, the barbaric practice of slavery was permitted under the Constitution in order to keep the slave-owning states in the union.

In retrospect, it would have behooved the Constitutional Convention to remember that when the issue of slavery was considered, "He that takes the devil in his boat, must carry him across the water." The price paid for this compromise was the tragedy of the Civil War.

Greater Personal Autonomy

There is, as discussed previously, one final distinction that deserves mention. The present book also argues that the acknowledgment and broadening of the liberty of conscience is yet another instance of a general trend toward the expansion of personal autonomy. In this respect, it can be classed with other movements that have claimed greater and greater independence from authority, both ancient and omnipresent. Science, voting, representative forms of government, and so forth, are obvious examples. The liberty of conscience fits within this mold because it recognizes the capacity for the self-determination of the individual, based on careful deliberation, of the relevant personal choices. Though family, religion, education, literature, the arts, and science all undoubtedly shape our manner of thought, it is ultimately the individual who must navigate these sources and influences to effectuate beliefs and behaviors. Even though the science of cognition can explain the mechanics of how we think, remember, or forget, there is still some schema against which we make distinctions between right and wrong, benefit and liability, and achievement and failure. The present book designates this process of evaluation and interpretation as the conscience.

The point here, is that reliance on a personal conscience has progressively gained in significance as the U.S. populace has experienced greater and greater freedom and autonomy. We rely much more on our consciences than we do on ancient texts and authorities. Therefore, to limit the right of conscience to religion would be analogous to limiting the mode of transportation to horseback. Clearly, much has happened in the course of the twentieth and twenty-first centuries to make the total reliance on either obsolete.

Perhaps this is the reason that Madison distinguished two types of conscience to begin with: religious and secular. Protecting the secular version, which amounts to protecting the right to think, choose, and judge, is the necessary prerequisite to an independent way of life.

Though the topic of conscience has been a central focus of this book as it relates to romance in the ivory tower, alternative concepts for representing deeply held personal perspectives also exist. Kent Greenawalt suggests, for example, something called the *comprehensive view*. A view is comprehensive to the extent that it incorporates all of the relevant principles and influences that determine a particular perspective, including beliefs and behaviors. Equal standing is given to secular and religious convictions, especially as they relate to the broader political landscape. The comprehensive view is thus yet another way of conceptualizing the step toward greater personal autonomy, and gives equal weight to religious and nonreligious frames of mind.

Besides his comprehensive view, Greenawalt's opinions about harm and homosexuality deserve mention as well. They are, surprisingly, similar to those asserted above. Greenawalt states:

I assume that in a liberal democratic society neither officials or citizens should seek legal prohibitions of actions simply because they are regarded as sins. Such prohibitions, as I argue in a previous book, lie too close to imposing religious views themselves on people to be proper. Thus, someone should not urge that consenting homosexual acts be penalized solely because she believes they are sins in the eyes of God or will bring bad consequences in an afterlife. The decisions on prohibition should depend on harms and benefits that are comprehensible in nonreligious terms in this life. Is this principle important at this stage of history? Rarely will anyone say an action is sinful despite its doing no damage in human terms. Nevertheless, the principle sets an important limit on appropriate justifications; and, by suggesting that arguments must be in terms of harms in the here and now, the principle can have practical effects. Its required reference to damages on this earth can significantly affect the weight of argument for and against a prohibition.[21]

Though consensus obviously does not preclude error, it does nonetheless increase confidence, if the opinions are independent and derived from different vantage points. Suffice it to say that Greenawalt has waded, at least briefly, into the waters examined here.

The psychoanalytic concept of the superego is also worthy of scrutiny, for at least two reasons. It is, first of all, premised on autonomy. The superego is the psychologically internal manifestation of the parent (both in the real and symbolic senses). In this respect, it is also the conscience—forever at watch, relentlessly involved.

Second, the superego, like psychoanalysis itself, shares much in common with religion, perhaps to the detriment of both. Here is the curious paradox.

Though ostensibly a science, psychoanalysis unfortunately has a fundamental scientific flaw: its core beliefs are immune to criticism and modification thereafter. Faith, instead, is just as essential to psychoanalysis as to religion itself.

This raises an interesting point. What if instead of religious freedom, the First Amendment afforded special protections to psychoanalytic beliefs, but not other equally tenable schools of thought? "Denial in the service of the ego," "the child is father to the man," the "id, ego, and superego," and other cherished psychoanalytic clauses would have constitutional standing, but alternative psychological perspectives, religions, and world-views would not.

Would the U.S. populace tolerate this? The answer is obvious: it would not. Perhaps it is easier to see the sheer folly of something when a substitution is made. Most people would not want a country steeped in constitutionally protected psychoanalysis, at the exclusion of all other points of view. The problem, however, is that it is extraordinarily difficult for Americans to realize that a sizable portion of the country feels the same way about constitutionally privileged religion. Giving preference to a particular point of view, whatever that point of view, always creates injustice. Religion fails to appreciate its stronghold on the U.S. people because its vast constituency supports its preferential treatment.

This is exactly what Madison and Jefferson fought so hard to avoid: a religious majority that either actively or inadvertently tyrannizes the religiously disinclined.

Which brings us, once again, to the issue at hand. The U.S. Constitution and U.S. jurisprudence were both built on a limited form of government that recognized substantial rights retained by the people—prominently, the rights and liberty of conscience, as evident in the constitutional archives. Though co-opted by religion, it is now time to return it to the people—most notably including consenting adults on college campuses.

Conclusion

All We Need Is Love (Love Is All We Need)

There is a scene in the movie *Miss Congeniality* in which beauty pageant contestants must make a speech. In doing so, each contestant dutifully praises "world peace," garnering instant applause from the audience. When, however, it is Sandra Bullock's turn, she instead rails about criminal injustice, which stuns the audience into silence. Beating a hasty retreat, Bullock extols world peace, whereupon the audience, sufficiently pleased, bursts into applause.

The word *religion*, paradoxically, has the same power on the Supreme Court. The Court, too, inevitably bursts into applause when the word is revealed. Mention a strongly held belief, follow it with the word religion, and constitutional magic will occur. The full force of the United States constitution protects it thereafter.

This process is no less transparent then the comical scene in *Miss Congeniality*. The joke works because it is readily apparent that it is entirely scripted. Applause in the movie is given if, and only if, the magical words are uttered.

Religion, it now seems, has been reduced to the same silly mantra. The very process designed to protect it has been humbled instead. Though a national religion has not been established, we have instead created a *nation* of religion in lieu of it. This, clearly, is in violation of the original intent.

Several decades ago John Lennon and Paul McCartney opined, "All you need is love. Love is all you need." It is a deeply cherished sentiment but, for the most part, wholly unrealistic.

Religion, in many respects, is a similar sentiment, with the equivalent pitfalls. "All you need is religion. Religion is all you need" is wonderfully optimistic but dreadfully oppressive as well. Given our devotion to liberty and freedom, something more than religion is obviously needed to protect the rights of conscience, particularly as they relate to sex and romance.

What, then, is the solution?

It would be useful, as a start, to implement the following suggestions introduced by Richard Posner, an appellate court justice himself. They refer to the need for the Supreme Court to formulate a coherent body of constitutional doctrine to decide issues of sexual autonomy. Two strategies are offered:

One is an inclination to approach questions of policy in a secular spirit, receptive to utilitarian, pragmatic and scientific arguments. The other is a willingness to invalidate state or federal laws on constitutional grounds without insisting that the invalidation be firmly grounded in the text of the Constitution.[1]

These strategies, obviously, are in the same spirit as those offered here, with one major exception. The present book also asserts that the text of the Constitution, the Ninth Amendment in particular, and more explicitly, the constitutional archives, provide firm grounding for consensual romantic and sexual rights (as retained by the people), and more deeply, as choices derived from the liberty of conscience.

It is, at last, the position of this book that the ultimate potential of the United States still rides firmly on the Constitution and its accompanying principles and archives. The ideas presented here are offered solely to further that objective, so that the U.S. populace can receive all that the Constitution was designed to give, including consenting adults on college campuses, who have the right, indisputably, to choose whom to romance, and to act on that choice.

Notes

Introduction

1. B. Miles, *Ginsberg* (New York: Harper, 1989), 492–493.

2. T. Bartlett, "The Question of Sex between Professors and Students," *Chronicle of Higher Education*, April 5, 2002, available at ⟨http:www.chronicle.com/weekly⟩.

3. P. Dilger, "Putting an End to Risky Romance," *Yale Magazine* 61, no. 6, April 1998.

4. J. Gallop, *Accused of Sexual Harassment* (Durham, NC: Duke University Press, 1997).

5. D. R. Euben, "Sexual Harassment in the Academy: Some Solutions for Faculty Policies and Procedures," American Association of University Professors, October 2002, available at ⟨http: www.aaup.org⟩.

6. N. Strossen, *Defending Pornography: Free Speech, Sex, and the Fight for Women's Rights* (New York: Scribner, 1995).

7. For the theoretical basis of this, see C. A. MacKinnon, *Sexual Harassment of Working Women: A Case of Sex Discrimination* (New Haven, CT: Yale University Press, 1979).

8. G. E. Elliot, "Consensual Relationships and the Constitution: A Case of Liberty Denied," *Michigan Journal of Gender and Law* 6 (1999), available at ⟨http://www.students.law.umich.edu⟩; P. Secunda, "Getting to the Nexus of the Matter: A Sliding Scale Approach to Faculty-Student Consensual Relationship Policies in Higher Education," *Syracuse Law Review* 55 (2004), available at ⟨http://www.law.syr.edu⟩; S. Young, "Getting to Yes: The Case

against Banning Consensual Relationships in Higher Education," *American University Journal of Gender and Law* 4 (1996), available at ⟨http://www.wcl.american.edu⟩.

9. Young, "Getting to Yes."

10. L. Jorgenson and R. M. Randles, "The Statute of Limitations and Fiduciary Theory in Psychotherapist Sexual Misconduct Cases," *Oklahoma Law Review* 181 (1991): 203–222.

11. Young, "Getting to Yes."

12. Elliot, "Consensual Relationships and the Constitution."

13. P. R. Abramson, S. D. Pinkerton, and M. Huppin, *Sexual Rights in America: The Ninth Amendment and the Pursuit of Happiness* (New York: New York University Press, 2003).

14. H. Friedrich, *Montaigne* (Berkeley: University of California Press, 1991), 26.

15. Abramson, Pinkerton, and Huppin, *Sexual Rights in America.*

Chapter 1

1. T. Paine, "Common Sense," in *The Thomas Paine Reader* (New York: Penguin, 1987), 91.

2. A. Koch, *Madison's "Advice to My Country"* (Princeton, NJ: Princeton University Press, 1966), 62.

3. S. Rabin-Margalioth, "Love at Work," *Duke Journal of Gender Law and Policy* 13, no. 296 (2006): 237–253.

4. H. P. Amaral, "Workplace Romance and Fraternization Policies," *Schmidt Labor Research Seminar Research Series* (2006): 1–25.

5. Rabin-Margalioth, "Love at Work"; Amaral, "Workplace Romance."

6. S. Young, "Getting to Yes: The Case against Banning Consensual Relationships in Higher Education," *American University Journal of Gender and Law* 4 (1996); G. E. Elliott, "Consensual Relationships and the Constitution: A Case of Liberty Denied," *Michigan Journal of Gender and Law* 6; P. M. Secunda, "Getting to the Nexus of the Matter: A Sliding Scale Approach to Faculty-Student Consensual

Relationship Policies in Higher Education," *Syracuse Law Review* 56 (1994), available at ⟨http://www.law.syr.edu⟩.

7. Young, "Getting to Yes."

8. Ibid.

9. C. MacKinnon, *Sexual Harassment of Working Women: A Case of Sex Discrimination* (New Haven, CT: Yale University Press, 1979).

10. P. R. Abramson and S. D. Pinkerton, *With Pleasure: Thoughts on the Nature of Human Sexuality* (New York: Oxford University Press, 1995).

11. Rabin-Margoliath, "Love at Work"; Amaral, "Workplace Romance."

12. M. Loftus, "Frisky Business: Romance in the Workplace," *Psychology Today* (1995), available at ⟨http://www.psychologytoday .com⟩.

13. Amaral, "Workplace Romance."

14. Consensual Relationships Policy, University of Wisconsin at Madison, available at ⟨http://www.oed.wisc.edu/sexualharassment/ policy⟩.

15. Policy on Teacher-Student Consensual Relations, Yale University, available at ⟨http://www.yale.edu/yalecollege/publications/instructors/ policy/harassment⟩.

16. P. R. Abramson, S. D. Pinkerton, and M. Huppin, *Sexual Rights in America: The Ninth Amendment and the Pursuit of Happiness* (New York: New York University Press, 2003).

17. UCLA Faculty Code of Conduct, part 2, section A.

18. The discussion of the University of California faculty-student dating policy is an elaboration of a commentary by Paul Abramson published in the *Los Angeles Times* on June 18, 2003. The commentary, in turn, was an extension of a position statement by Abramson and Keith Holyoak, both professors in the psychology department at UCLA, that was submitted to a vice chancellor to challenge the romance policy, but was ignored by the academic senate and administration, because the policy itself had been approved in principle prior to the request for feedback.

19. I want to emphasize the word *potentially* because there are no data that the prohibition of romance or sex between faculty and

students reduces either the incidence or costs of sexual harassment lawsuits on university campuses.

20. Abramson, Pinkerton, and Huppin, *Sexual Rights in America.*

21. Secunda, "Getting to the Nexus of the Matter."

22. Letter from James Madison to Thomas Jefferson, May 13, 1798, in J. M. Smith, *The Republic of Letters: The Correspondence between Jefferson and Madison* (New York: W. W. Norton, 1995), 1048.

23. C. G. Haines, *The Role of the Supreme Court in American Government and Politics, 1789–1835* (Berkeley: University of California Press, 1944), 159. I am also indebted to this source for much of the background material on the early years of the Supreme Court.

24. M. D. Peterson, "Alien and Sedition Acts," in *The First Amendment*, ed. K. Karst (New York: Macmillan, 1986).

25. N. Hentoff, *The First Freedom: The Tumultuous History of Free Speech in America* (New York: Dell, 1980).

26. Haines, *The Role of the Supreme Court*, 164.

27. Thomas Jefferson to Martha Jefferson Randolph, May 17, 1798, Edgehill-Randolph Papers, University of Virginia.

28. Smith, *The Republic of Letters*, 1064.

29. Ibid.

30. Ibid., 1065.

31. Ibid., 1069.

32. J. Madison, *Writings* (Washington, DC: Library of America, 1999), 648–649.

33. Ibid., 649–650.

34. Ibid., 650.

35. Ibid., 647.

36. Ibid., 633.

37. Ibid., 645.

38. Ibid., 645.

39. Ibid., 656.

40. Ibid., 656.

41. Ibid., 657.

42. N. H. Cogan, *The Complete Bill of Rights* (New York: Oxford University Press, 1997), 1.

43. *New York Times Co. v. Sullivan*, 376 U.S. 254 (1964), argued January 6, 1964, decided March 9, 1964 by vote of nine to zero.

44. Ibid., 276.

45. Ibid., 269.

46. Ibid., 271–272.

47. Ibid., 270.

48. Letter from Thomas Jefferson to Edward Dowse, April 19, 1803. The Thomas Jefferson Papers, Series 1. General Correspondence. ⟨http: www.memory.loc.gov/⟩.

Chapter 2

1. T. Potts, *Conscience in Medieval Philosophy* (Cambridge: Cambridge University Press, 1980).

2. J. D. Douglas, F. F. Bruce, J. I. Packer, N. Hillyer, N. Guthrie, A. R. Millard, and D. J. Wiseman, *New Bible Dictionary* (Leicester, UK: Inter-varsity Press, 1982).

3. P. Miller, *Roger Williams: His Contribution to the American Tradition* (New York: Atheneum, 1962), 62.

4. Ibid., 62.

5. Ibid., 62.

6. C. G. Pestana, *Liberty of Conscience and the Growth of Religious Diversity in Early America, 1636–1786* (Providence, RI: John Carter Brown Library, 1986), 38.

7. E. S. Morgan, *Roger Williams: The Church and the State* (New York: W. W. Norton, 1967), 25.

8. Ibid., 25.

9. Ibid., 36.

10. E. S. Gaustad, *Liberty of Conscience: Roger Williams in America* (Grand Rapids, MI: Erdmans, 1991), 147.

11. Miller, *Roger Williams*, chapters 1, 2, 4.

12. J. Locke, *Works*, 11th ed. (London: W. Otridge and Sons, 1812), 10:317. Cited in E. Leites, "Casuistry and Character," in *Conscience*

and Casuistry in Early Modern Europe, ed. E. Leites (Cambridge: Cambridge University Press, 2002), 120.

13. J. Sharp, *Theological Works* (Oxford: Oxford University Press, 1892), 2:192, 2:186–188. Cited and paraphrased in Leites, "Casuistry and Character," 127.

14. L. Busher, "Religion's Peace: A Plea for the Liberty of Conscience" (1614), in *Tracts on Liberty of Conscience and Persecution, 1614–1661*, ed. E. B. Underhill (1846; repr., Boston: Adamant Media Corporation, 2005), 27.

15. Cited in Leites, "Casuistry and Character," 121.

16. Ibid.

17. *Abraham Lincoln's Great Speeches* (New York: Dover, 1991), 103.

18. J. S. Mill, *On Liberty* (1859, repr., Indianapolis, IN: Hackett, 1978), 9.

19. I. Berlin, *Four Essays on Liberty* (Oxford: Oxford University Press, 1969), 121–122.

20. P. R. Abramson, S. D. Pinkerton, and M. Huppin, *Sexual Rights in America: The Ninth Amendment and Pursuit of Happiness* (New York: New York University Press, 2003).

21. Ibid.

22. J. Rawls, *A Theory of Justice* (Cambridge, MA: Harvard University Press, 1971), 202.

23. Ibid., 207.

24. Cited in J. L. Clayton, "The Supreme Court, Polygamy, and the Enforcement of Morals in Nineteenth-Century America: An Analysis of *Reynolds v. United States*," in *Conscience and Belief: The Supreme Court and Religion*, ed. K. L. Hal (New York: Garland, 2000), 48.

25. Ibid.

26. Clayton, "The Supreme Court," 50.

27. *Reynolds v. the United States*, 98 U.S. 148 (1878).

28. Clayton, "The Supreme Court," 50.

29. T. Jefferson, "Notes on the State of Virginia" (1787), in *Writings* (New York: Library of America, 1984), 285.

30. Ibid., 286.

31. Clayton, "The Supreme Court," 64.

32. Clayton, "The Supreme Court," 58–73.

33. *United States v. Ballard*, 322 U.S. 78 (1944).

34. Cited in M. R. Konvitz, *Religious Liberty and Conscience* (New York: Viking, 1968).

35. J. D'Emilio and E. B. Freedman, *Intimate Matters: A History of Sexuality in America* (New York: Harper and Row, 1988), 181.

36. P. R. Abramson and S. D. Pinkerton, *With Pleasure: Thoughts on the Nature of Human Sexuality* (New York: Oxford University Press, 1995).

Chapter 3

1. T. Jefferson, "Notes on the State of Virginia" (1787), in *Writings* (New York: Library of America, 1984), 285.

2. Ibid., 510.

3. T. Jefferson, "A Bill for Establishing Religious Freedom," in *Writings* (New York: Library of America, 1984), 347.

4. N. H. Cogan, *The Complete Bill of Rights* (New York: Oxford University Press, 1997), 1.

5. Ibid., 2.

6. Ibid., 2.

7. M. McConnell, "The Origins and Historical Understanding of Free Exercise of Religion," *Harvard Law Review* 103 (1990): 1409–1517.

8. Cogan, *The Complete Bill of Rights*, 12.

9. Ibid., 15.

10. Ibid, 12.

11. Ibid., 12.

12. Ibid., 22.

13. Ibid., 51.

14. Ibid., 47.

15. Ibid., 48.

16. Letter from Janes Madison to Thomas Jefferson, May 13, 1798, in J. M. Smith, *The Republic of Letters: The Correspondence between Jefferson and Madison* (New York: W. W. Norton, 1995), 1562.

17. P. R. Abramson, S. D. Pinkerton, and M. Huppin, *Sexual Rights in America: The Ninth Amendment and the Pursuit of Happiness* (New York: New York University Press, 2003).

18. R. Godbeer, *Sexual Revolution in Early America* (Baltimore: Johns Hopkins University Press, 2002), 300–301.

19. J. Madison, *Notes on Debates in the Federal Convention* (1840; repr., New York: W. W. Norton, 1987), 478.

20. Ibid., 486.

21. K. Greenawalt, *Private Consciences and Public Reasons* (New York: Oxford University Press, 1995), 6.

Conclusion

1. R. A. Posner, *Sex and Reason* (Cambridge, MA: Harvard University Press, 1992), 350.

Index